Remember The Carrot

A Change of Pace on the Appalachian Trail

Aaron Welch

Published by
CreateSpace
Scotts Valley, CA

Manufactured in the United States of America.

Cover photo by Roger "Apple" Morse. Book design by Aaron Welch.

ISBN 144047799X   EAN 9781440477997

Dedicated to

Debra, my wife;
Roger ("Apple"), my best man;
and the AT Class of 2000.

Preface

A Foreword

L ike a hiking trail, the mind winds up in new places while discovering new things and going to new levels. Just as no landscape is the same from mountain to mountain on the Appalachian Trail, the human mind seems to evolve and change in time.

I would like the reader to know that the thoughts, feelings, and catharses written about in this book were experiences for the Trail, and the seasons of my mind have changed in time, and I do not necessarily think or believe in the same ways described in these pages. My wish, however, is that you also allow yourself to go to different places when reading this book—whether in vicarious adventure of body or imagination... and then to move on.

Aaron Welch
October 1, 2008

Oh, by the way... Be sure to check out the color photos on my Website: **www.rememberthecarrot.com**, where also you can order *Remember The Carrot* shirts, mugs, hats, bookmarks, clocks, extra copies of the book, and even a downloadable version!

Contents

It were as well
to be educated in the shadow
of a mountain as in more classic shade.
Some will remember, no doubt,
not only that they went to college,
but that they went to the mountain.

HENRY DAVID THOREAU

An old-fashioned Appalachian Trail blaze.

Pre-Trail Tidbit
Trial by Fire

Yeah, I was booted from a Christian magazine publisher. But as I saw it, *I* wasn't terminated—my employment was. I had been postmarked: "Return to Sender," just in time for Thanksgiving.

To me, an occupation was what occupied my time, while I figured out how I was going to have *enough* time and money to enjoy life. My former occupation was actually a *preoccupation* with money, status, power, and reputation. I wanted more out of life than those trappings. This was ironic to me, considering that I'd worked for a company who believed they administered the Truth. But I felt backward and cut off from life and reality. I longed to get down to earth; to reintroduce myself to Mother Nature. Mother Culture, however, told me to stick to her rules.

"Money, status, power, reputation… Everyone's doing it," she said. "It's the only way, it's the real world."

I didn't believe her. Wishing to cancel my subscription to the Rat Race & Hubbub, I wondered why everyone I knew seemed to subscribe to it at any cost. My worldview was wilting, as a passion for adventure was sprouting. And my white collar loosened and fell like dried petals to the ground.

During that Thanksgiving weekend, an idea blossomed to hike the

Appalachian Trail from beginning to end: a thru-hike, so it's called, from Springer Mountain, Georgia to Mount Katahdin, Maine. And why not start the following March? I had found the jigsaw puzzle's missing piece!

Blooming with giddiness, I blew hundreds of dollars on equipment, having never backpacked in my life. I knew nothing about gear and long-distance hiking. Thus, when my bank account dwindled, my rationale drew interest: *What if hiking the Appalachian Trail isn't the right thing for me to do at this point in my life? Was my impulsiveness a sign that it is indeed the wrong time to hike?* My pastor persuaded me not to go.

"You really need to settle down," he said.

"Settle down?" I said with a huff. "What for?"

"It would be good for you. Spend a few years at something productive."

"A few years, eh? What in the world would be worth my spending that amount of time on?"

"Go back to school and finish your degree." He shrugged. "Get a promising job."

I bit my tongue. *How novel,* I thought. My stomach turned, as I gulped his murky potion, spooned to me on behalf of good intent. I popped my knuckles one by one. *Maybe my pastor is right: Life was meant, by God, to be found in civilized work and production. Besides, I have been reckless.* Now I didn't trust myself. So, with a sigh I took a raincheck on the Appalachian Trail, and I tried to forget about hiking it. I tackled another job, waiting tables, which gave me the flexibility to do what little I could to enjoy the outdoors—even in the Chicago 'burbs.

My world continued to crumble. Unhappiness, taxes, bills, and panic wrapped their nasty fingers around me, taking their toll. I came to believe that control and freedom were illusions, while piles of frustration and doubt heaped higher around me. And God? Was he as illusory? Was it possible that we'd created him in *our* image as an attempt to reach back for that lost freedom and control? What was I missing?

The following spring and summer, I loosed my tension on local trails, stomping bitterness and dread into the dirt. Cattails knelt over the marshy trail. I smacked them away, cracking their reeds. Cottonseed clouds poofed into the air. I shooed them away and mulled forward until my legs petered out. Under a shade tree I paused for rest, but my mind chugged onward. *Run!* it screamed. *Run away! Run!* But I couldn't run—my life was stuck in the goop of depression. I kicked back with my head in my folded hands, and I peered up into the branches, where the sunlight trickled through.

"If trees could talk," I said to myself, "what would they say? Why do they seem so happy, so content, so at home?"

A heavy gloom pulled my eyelids closed like window shades, and I dozed off as my mind echoed, "Why do I constantly feel at odds with the world?"

As I lay in the grass, my feet twitched and burrowed deep into the soil. Each toe then split into two and grew fatter and longer, rooting in every direction. I felt no pain; it was a dream. When I stood up, I could see the cattail pond in the distance and a trail winding around the forest. A bird landed on my arm, which was covered in leaves. Each of my fingers had also doubled and had sprouted branches and limbs. I was planted. I was a tree. I was happy.

In my mind, many seasons passed. Spring gave gifts of joy and vitality. Summer brought strength and endurance. In autumn, I gave back to the Earth whatever I could in thanksgiving before winter gave me rest and confidence. The winds carried wisdom. I loved being a tree.

The next summer, a breeze brought with it a faint voice. *Mumbles and grumbles,* I thought, *it can only be a human's voice.* I waved back and forth to look for the human and found him at the cattail pond. Poor cattails. Oh, how they howled when the human beat them, but he couldn't hear them. Poor boy. He looked so sad. I covered him with my arms as he lay down next to me.

"Sleep. Go to sleep," I whispered. Every tree knows that in Dreamland humans hear our voices better. I wanted to speak to him.

His eyes closed.

"Why do I constantly feel at odds with the world?" he moaned.

"Perhaps 'your world' was never really intact to begin with," I answered.

His mind's eyes opened, and he continued, "I feel like I'm trapped in a cage. How will I ever fit into this 'bigger, better, faster' mentality? Not to mention God and Christian thought."

I felt his pain and understood his questions. "Do you *want* to remain within your rigid boundaries?" I asked. "Or do you want to venture out and to think anew; to go outside the box that's been tacked together for you to thrive in?"

"I want out. But I'm afraid it won't be easy," he said.

"Easy? Sure, thinking inside the box is less painful. It's *easier* not to question anything. But life is bigger, full of wonder and delight," I said.

The human tossed around. "Easy for you to say. You've got everything you need for happiness right here."

"You're right," I replied. "And so do you."

"Come on! Look at me. I'm a mess."

"The cattails also have everything they need for happiness," I said. "They have something special for their needs. When you think about it, you have that very same thing."

5

"What is this, a riddle? What do I have in common with a cattail?" the human asked.

"The cattail seeds on your shirt show the answer," I said.

A little smile opened on the human's face. "Ah, I get it. A mode of transportation."

"That's it," I replied. "When it's time, the cattail lets the wind carry it on to new adventures. The cattail's seeds are its way of moving onward. It's a built-in happiness mechanism. Your mechanism is your legs. Use them. Walk away from your box. Find a happiness that works for you."

"But aren't I supposed to find happiness, wonder, and delight from inside my box?" the human cried.

"Perhaps you're just not made for that box," I said, dropping a couple of leaves on him. "You want something fresh. A new box, a renewed spirit."

"Oh, yes, but where do I go for that? And how do I patch up the mess I'm in?" he said.

It seemed simple to me. "Fix nothing. But go and seek firmer ground." I reached down and tickled his face with a leaf.

He woke up.

When I awoke, I opened my eyes and sat up. The shade had stepped aside, leaving me in the sunlight. I sighed. "If trees could talk..."

I picked up a vibrant green leaf sitting next to me. And a sense of urgency poured over me to throw my box away or to take what I had and stretch the box's borders; to push out the sides of the box and allow exploration for this madly curious mind of mine. The desire to hike the Appalachian Trail, pushed to a back burner, was simmering again.

Another leaf drifted down from the tree. I sucked in a chest full of air and marveled at the perfect tune of everything around me. It was as if I'd turned over a new leaf. I waved my arms around the forest and exclaimed, "This really works! I really work! This *all* really works—functions—together. Perfectly!"

Brushing up against leaves and cattails now felt as though they were showing affection for me. They were no longer an intrusion or a nuisance to my selected route. Instead of shoving them aside, I let them fall on my face and hands like a kiss. They were real and alive, created from the ground up, just as I was. Amazement tugged at my tear ducts, and I felt that I'd found where I belonged: in the outdoors. No longer would I settle for what I thought was less. I wanted a new direction, a "road less traveled."

The smoldering Appalachian Trail flickered into a raging flame, bringing to a boil the need to hike it. I would begin thru-hiking next spring, just a few months away. My entire being was ignited, "and there was light," that first day. It was a light bulb switching on before the end of a torturously long tunnel.

Although journeys of "a thousand miles begin with a single step," I knew that a trek of Appalachian magnitude must begin with a new spirit *and* lots of planning. I read everything I could get my hands on from the Trail's history and geology to its political and wildlife backgrounds. I reckoned that it might be just as important to scout out equipment and learn how to use it. *What are all those straps and things on my backpack for, anyhow? How should I dress for the occasion? And what, by Jove, am I going to eat?*

Despite the everlasting wrestle through the Rat Race, my blue-collar petals had now wilted, and I stepped onto a Greyhound bus for Georgia. Was I prepped and primed? I hoped so. Did I have all the essential gear? Yes. Did I know what I was doing? Not really. Did I have enough money even to get me through? I'd heard it said that a thru-hiker should count on $1.50 for every mile of the Trail. I had less money than that, but determination worth its weight in gold. This wasn't about money, anyhow. It was about finding my way.

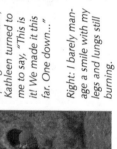

Top Left: I still recall the tourists at Amicalola Falls. They had no idea what I was in for.

Bottom Left: On Springer Mountain, Kathleen turned to me to say, "This is it! We made it this far. One down..."

Right: I barely manage a smile with my legs and lungs still burning.

Trail Tidbit #1
Outrunning Rats

Twenty-one hours in a stuffy Greyhound bus reminded me of being back in an office full of cramped cubicles... only this one with its own port-o-potty. Nevertheless, whereas the finish line in the Rat Race seems forever distant, Gainesville, Georgia was a goal in sight. Snapping through the ribbon at the finish line wouldn't be the end, however. I imagined it was actually like cutting the ribbon at the opening-ceremony for a new monument.

Exiting the bus at the Gainesville Greyhound station, I sucked in a deep breath of hot Georgian air, a pleasant change from the Midwest's seasonal chill. My loaded backpack served as a chair, as I awaited my shuttle to the Approach Trail at Amicalola Falls State Park. Already my mind began to wander through the hills, fantasizing about my next few thousand steps, the lullabies at night by swaying trees, and peacefu–

"Pardon me, are you Aaron?" called the Greyhound fare lady with a southern-fried accent. "I have a message from the Rasmussens that they're runnin' late. But they're still comin' fer ya." I had phoned Mr. and Mrs. Rasmussen a week earlier, in response to their online advertisement for rides to the trailhead.

Under sultry sunbeams, I looked again at the reflection of my dreams in the puddles of my flash-flooding worldview. Drowning out the world around me,

I began to relax... until a man floated up to me.

"Excuse me," he interrupted, "I'm a positive thinker."

So it said on his lapel pin, too.

Cheesy, I thought, *you're excused.*

A homemade business card dropped into my palm, as he explained why I should ring him up when I was finished with the Trail. His work in a multilevel marketing sales job vended litigation insurance. It was another spoonful to jamb into my stuffed belly, and I told him that I wasn't hungry; that I was trying to flush out of my life this toxic sense of power and control over a sugar-cereal empire.

"So, you're basically taking advantage of people's legal paranoia?" I asked. "No thank you, I'm not interested." I'd heard lawyers being labeled "dirty rats," and his morsel of cheese certainly didn't entice me to step back into the Rat Race with them to munch it. I returned to my spot on the curbside to meditate. Ah, the warm sun.

Moments later, yet another man chimed in. "Sir, do you have any spare change?" he asked, "I need to make a phone call."

Befuddled, I blinked several times, picked my pockets, and handed the Mexican fellow some coins. His long, black hair hung as limp as the look on his face.

"Gracias," he murmured. "My name is Jerry."

We chatted for a while until he was picked up. Jerry's journey would lead him to a drug rehabilitation center. I cheered him on, hoping he would cross his finish line, too.

Again, I lost myself in introspection, as cars zipped by, and people darted to and fro, as if the sun were hustling to set forever. It was a tug-of-war contest for my attention.

"Hello, Mr. Welch?" someone beckoned another hour later. It was My Fare Lady again with her heavy accent. "The Rasmussens called again, and said they're on their way."

When Mr. and Mrs. Rasmussen arrived, they apologized for being late. "We had sewer problems," they said.

"Don't worry about it," I snickered, climbing into the Jeep. "I'm in no rush." *Leave racing to the racers*, I thought, *my racing days are over.*

Trail Tidbit #2
Salutations

Months of grooming and headwork for the Trail drifted aside, as I solemnly stood at the Approach Trail's gate, 8.8 miles away from Springer Mountain, the southern terminus, where Appalachian Trail northbounders would see their first blaze. There was no pep talk or cheering—only the invitation of somber, whispering trees. I was alone, but not lonely; not anxious, but eager; pensive. *Where would this path lead me?* As I staggered up the first slope, such moods stepped aside, making way for my panting lungs to get a thought in edgewise: *More air!*

The purpose of those first miles to Springer Mountain, I swear, was to weed out people, who were not so serious about the task after all. Up and up downed my energy quickly because of the drawn-out bus ride, so I retired just shy of Springer Mountain at Nimblewill Gap. I'd greet Springer first thing the next morning. Setting camp, cooking dinner, I enjoyed the blazing sunset as it cast rich hues onto Earth. Everything glowed an iridescent red, as if I were on Mars with trees. The sun cradled herself behind the distant purple mountain majesties.

I awoke the next morning ready to introduce myself to Springer Mountain. My first acquaintance, however, was prospective thru-hiker Kathleen. Together we hit the Appalachian Trail's first peak, as the thrill of the moment soared like rockets. Despite rubbery legs, we made a successful liftoff. Light rain met us at the top, but didn't snuff out our fires. We posed for snapshots at the summit's plaque, where we reverently touched the first white blaze—the two-by-six inch painted mark of the "AT". It would become a narcissistic friend, whose portrait might appear on any tree, rock, or post from here to moose country.

Mile after mile of the Trail sparkled underfoot with bits of mica, a glassy mineral common to the area. Fascinated by the mica's flat shiny surface, we were walking as if on a broken mirror. Kathleen picked up a piece and said, "I could do my make-up in this!"

Experts call the Appalachians the oldest mountains in the world, once higher than the Himalayas. Areas of original bedrock in the Great Smokies could be as old as one billion years old. A sense of wonder and intrigue trickled through my veins, as my body mingled with such ancient land—let alone with the single path that stretched over 2,167 miles ahead of me all the way to Maine. I found myself smitten with love at first sight of the Trail's own dwelling place.

One veteran hiker, Godspeed, had told me, "Remember, the Trail is like a fine wine. It gets better and more valuable as time passes." When the first day on the Appalachian Trail came to a close, I was game for another wine. I had already tasted some of its sweetness: mountain overlooks, long tunnels through rhododendron greens, virgin hemlock groves, and new friends.

Sprawled out like a pile of dirty laundry in my sleeping bag that night, I spied a mouse scurrying over my tent-rooftop. It reminded me of my Mickey Mouse life amidst the concrete and car exhaust, computers and crowds, preoccupation and restlessness. But quiet, dark bedtime hours in the barren mountain trees magically increased distances tenfold. Ten miles of Trail became one hundred in my soul. Feeling like I'd outrun the rats, I was free to look forward to tomorrow.

Trail Tidbit #3

For Crying Out Loud

Journal Entry
3/31/00—From Justus Creek Campsite to Burnett Field Mountain (12 miles)

Spring mountains don't seem to attract animals. Do they lack food? Perhaps warmer weather in lower altitudes allows more winter vegetation. Maybe there are too many hikers. So, while I hike the heights, apparently wildlife makes its habitat elsewhere. Nothing but scavenger birds circled all day, buzzards and crows… in all their glory!

Two nights ago, I met "Crying Wolf" and his dog Rowdy at Hawk Mountain Shelter. We camped behind it since it was jam-packed with snoring hikers. Our paces are similar, so we've seen a lot of each other.

Last night, Kathleen (my first new friend from Springer), Crying Wolf, and I enjoyed our campsite by Justus Creek, where the cool water was refreshing to wade in after that god-awful Sassafras Mountain. I'm not sure what's worse: straight up, or straight down. Such workouts make me starved by suppertime.

I invited Kathleen and Crying Wolf over to "my place" for dinner and hot drinks. Kathleen saves pack-weight by carrying cold food; that is, less fuel and no stove equals lighter backpack. But Crying Wolf and I flared up our Whisperlite one-pot stoves and boiled our Lipton noodles. This morning my stomach was still churning last night's dinner, so I had to force my oatmeal down. Kathleen says my appetite will become ravenous in a few short weeks.

Today, Kathleen started hiking later than Crying Wolf and I. Rowdy seemed to hike two miles around every one of ours, as she scampered ahead and back, up and down ridges. Crying Wolf told me how Natives once loved this particular area. A Georgian, he knows a lot about the region.

"Except for a po-dunk tourist trap on an Indian reservation in North Carolina," he said, "the Cherokees are gone from these hills. We got rid of them long ago. Such a damn shame."

Anything for the sake of Man-land, I thought, *White-man-land... in the name of God, no less.*

"But their spirits are here," Crying Wolf continued. "When the sound of water mixes with the wind, you can hear their voices."

I laughed but recalled how many times, when hiking alone, I thought I heard someone talking. I'd stop to listen and would only hear water gushing somewhere in the distance.

"Yeah, man! Them are spirits!" Crying Wolf barked in his Georgian drawl.

"Did you hear the coyotes yapping last night?" I asked him.

"Wasn't that great?" answered Crying Wolf.

"Fantastic! If I were alone, it might have freaked me out, but with other people in the area, I felt safe," I said.

"Man, I enjoyed the hell out of that!" he replied. I had to laugh again. Crying Wolf has a curious way of putting "hell" into odd places.

Soon Kathleen caught up to us at the Gooch Gap shelter spring (where we had stopped for water, and wherein Rowdy had sat to cool herself off—after our water was gathered). She asked for a Band-Aid for her blistered foot. Pulling off the shoe from her swollen foot, she announced her trailname.

"Lady Kat... with a 'K.' 'Kat' being short for Kathleen, or caterpillar because I'm so slow."

True, she isn't a swift hiker, but she can stack on the miles as well as anyone could. Her strength and tenacity thus far lead me to believe she'll see Maine.

"You know, Kathleen... I mean Lady Kat," I said, "'Kat' is also short for Katahdin."

"Right!" she said with beaming eyes.

"Hell, now *you* need a trailname." Crying Wolf pointed at me. "We'll work on it."

Just past Gooch Gap shelter, at a dirt road crossing, we found—Lo and behold!— a garbage bin! Crying Wolf was especially joyous over the occasion; he'd been waiting for days now to throw away his packed-out trash. While Lady Kat and I tossed our junk, Rowdy sat by and watched Crying Wolf tear apart his backpack, looking for his gallon-size Ziplock bag of garbage.

"Now, I know I put that where I could get at it," he exclaimed, digging deeper, dumbfounded. All the contents of his pack were flung about. A flying sock. A bouncing TP roll. Lady Kat and I waited patiently with granola bars in hand, as Crying Wolf unrolled his tent and crawled inside for a look-see. An airborne Ramen Noodles packet. A bundled bandana.

"I *think* I was conscious when I packed this morning," he said.

Rowdy seemed to shrug her furry shoulders and say, "Don't look at me!"

Crying Wolf weaseled out of his tent and stood among the gear strewn about him, pondering the predicament with his hands on his hips. A flipping expletive.

"Aw, hell!" he muttered in that all-too-familiar tone, which essentially meant, "I am such an idiot!" He cast a glare over to us and said, "I knew I put it where I could get it."

His garbage bag was strapped to the outside of his backpack. Lady Kat and I guffawed, as we turned to hike onward. Rowdy followed, smirking.

Crying Wolf shouted forth, "That's the last time I let my dog pack my bags!"

Left: Kathleen decided to camp alone at Long Creek Falls. Micah and I trodded farther before settling. The next day, Kathleen would say, "It'll be a while before I camp alone again; the coyotes spooked me all night long, and I'm not yet in good enough shape to run up these hills for help!"

Right: The hills gave birth to new lives, which set the Winter stage with drama. They were named Bloodroot.

Trail Tidbit #4
April Fools

The community of hikers was a subculture containing classes, cliques and customs of its own. Trekkers found their niches and bonded with others, feeling as if they'd been friends for years. Four days towards Maine, Crying Wolf, Lady Kat and I had already handled highs and lows together, and we joked and complained together.

Ah! Novelty was where it was at. When all was new and every experience fresh, virgin hikers like myself didn't mind eating clumpy oatmeal, tramping through rain, tolerating pests, or even climbing rocks instead of skirting ways around them. The Trail somehow formed a new matrix of time and energy in my mind, making me feel as if I'd been on the Trail for weeks. I assumed the position of a trail-hardened hiker. I *assumed* it. April Fools Day amended my constitution.

It started after I was tucked into my sleeping bag that first April eve. I was snug. A yawn and a stretch bade dreamtime to come and play. I tottered on the edge of sleep, ready to fall in, when a noise at the head of my tent flustered me.

Scritch, scritch...

"Wha-was-at?!" I jerked my head up. *Scritch, scritch...*

All I could think of was Crying Wolf's comment when Lady Kat and I were chatting about mice in the shelters, "Sometimes them critters'll crawl right underneath your tent!"

Gasp! I had just stupidly eaten inside my tent, *scritch, scritch…* and the mice must have smelled the food and were coming after me! *Scritch, scritch…*

"Ah! Oh!" I coughed. *Scritch, scritch…* There it was again. Under my tent!

"Omigosh! Move over, move over!"

I scooted to one side of the tent, farthest away from the intruder. *Scritch, scritch…*

It made its way towards the doorway of my tent, and I shone my flashlight through the no-see-um netting to expose the impostor.

"Huh? A b—a bug?!" I exclaimed. It was a frickin' insect! A big black bug. No mouse.

"April Fools!" it shouted.

Yes, I heard it loud as gunfire. It mocked me and my trail-hardened delusions. Frayed nerves could wear novelty out, after all.

Wallowing in my chagrin, I realized that I wasn't as ripe a hiker as I'd thought. It was like a kick in the butt. Petty concerns such as these would become mundane after some experience points, but for now I was indeed the April Fool. I had mountains to climb before I'd wise up, yet a kick in the butt *was* a step forward.

Trail Tidbit #5
Appalachian Appellation

Nicknaming is a steadfast tradition on the Appalachian Trail. Somewhere along the Trail, most hikers received a trailname, or as I tagged it, an "Appalachian Appellation." Anything from a personality trait to an odd habit, which a backpacker carried, would often come out of hiding with the special label. For example, "Deadman Walking" was nearly blind and hard of hearing; "Jester" was a zany wit; "Gigglebox" is self explanatory, and Hacksaw was a champion snorer. The roster is endless.

Although some hikers resisted being trail-dubbed, and others chose names for themselves, I couldn't wait to see what befell me. What mark would signify my Trail experience? Telling people my birth name was becoming awkward, like asking for a hot-dog at a posh restaurant after everyone else had ordered tuxedo food. But I was only one week past Springer Mountain, so I added a side order of patience, too.

Neither Crying Wolf nor Lady Kat had had any suggestions for my trailname. And now our trio had been split over Blood Mountain, the day before the perky weather turned sour. Too green at backpacking to handle such foul rains, my tender leaves got hammered. So I retreated to Whitley Gap shelter alone. A 64-year-old man was reclined within.

"Come on in out of the rain," he said. "I'm Just An Echo."

"Thanks. Great name," I said, unbuckling my hip-belt.

"What's yours?" he asked.

I gave him my name.

"That's your real name... Don't you have a trailname yet?"

"Oh, nope. Still looking and waiting," I answered.

"We'll remedy that," Echo promised, as he pulled out his notebook to share a list of names he'd collected over the years: Dances With Blisters, Dirt Mouth, Double Barrel, Slojourner....

"I just met Double Barrel and Slojourner yesterday on Blood Mountain," I gaped. "You met them, too?"

"Last year I did," said Just An Echo. "They were thru-hiking."

"That's right," I said. "They were just day-hiking yesterday and took me to a country restaurant for dinner."

"It's a small world," Echo said, stuffing his notebook back into his pack.

"So you were on the Trail last year, too?" I asked.

Just An Echo stifled a grin, gazed toward the ceiling, and humored me from the annals of echoes past.

"Well, I've hiked the Trail every year since 1994," he said, pausing for effect.

Sizing him up, I poked my eyes back into place and objected, "Every year since 19—"

"Well, I've never actually hiked the whole thing." he said, pleased to have caught me off guard. "I always mean to, but tend to get sidetracked by things."

I jerked my head back in the shape of a question mark.

He continued, "One year I hyper-extended my knee and broke my glasses. Another year I had to be rescued from hypothermia. Then there was the congestive heart failure. Sometimes I just had other appointments off-trail from which I simply never returned."

I admired his tenacity. He was like a rubberband attached to the Trail, always snapping back when pulled off.

Wet clothes hung from nails. Soupy clouds hung from treetops. A bashful silence hung between Echo and me for the rest of the day. I scribbled a note in the register, which every shelter had. Crying Wolf and Rowdy blew in with the thundering winds as dusk settled.

"Hey! Welcome home," I said from inside my toasty sleeping bag.

"Hell, I thought I lost you," Crying Wolf said.

"Come on in," Echo called.

Straggling behind Crying Wolf were new faces Tenderfoot, Lawrence and his wife. Lawrence spread out his sleeping pad and draped some dry clothes over a nail.

"I hope nobody's shy," he warned, facing away from us to peel off his dripping shorts and long-johns.

Tenderfoot blurted, "Wow! The 'moon' is out early tonight!"

"Aha! 'Moonchild' is your new name, Lawrence!" I declared, as he quickly yanked up some dry pants over his bare rump.

He decided that Moonchild sounded like something out of the '60s, so I suggested "Rising Moon." It was like playing "Pin the Tail on the Donkey," and in the end I stuck him with the label.

"Nice to meet you, Rising Moon, I'm Just An Echo," the quiet man lying in the corner piped up. "I'll have to write that one down. What's your wife's name?"

"My name's Erin," she said for herself.

"Hey, that's my name, too!" I remarked. "Only not spelled the same."

Rising Moon said, "Ha! It's a small world…"

"Hey! Small World!" hollered Echo, "That's you! Where's my notebook?"

Two baptisms in one day, it was confirmed. Because "Small World" was original and didn't contain the words feet, blisters, walking, or trail, I accepted it. I was trail-christened Small World, and my birth name was packed away, as another personal item to carry, rarely seen by others.

Top Left: Tenderfoot, Rising Moon, Erin, Chad, and Just-An-Echo (hand) acted like sardines in Whitley Gap shelter. Tenderfoot had cards; we played Go Fish.

Bottom Left: I stood proudly on the Sacred Oak.

Right: Crying Wolf pledged allegience to the Trail.

Trail Tidbit #6
Never Cry Wolf

Sunk between two steep mounts, Unicoi Gap was the end of the line for Crying Wolf's dog, Rowdy. She was dog-tired. Crying Wolf was sad to see her go. Among a dozen Boy Scouts, we waited for Crying Wolf's roommate, Brian, to come and pick her up. The sun pecked at our bodies for two hours, until it finally nested behind Rocky Mount, just as Brian's vehicle approached. We gathered our gear.

Brian parked behind the Scouts' van, intentionally concealing his surprise cargo from Crying Wolf's view. Smiles, handshakes, and introductions exchanged, Brian reached for our gear to stow in the Jeep.

"There's someone here to see you," Brian said to Crying Wolf.

"Oh, yeah? Who?" Crying Wolf asked, picking up his hiking sticks. Rounding into view from the Jeep came Bill. Jaw and sticks dropped. Crying Wolf hugged him with wholehearted cheer. "What the hell are you doing here?" he asked with a blast of laughter.

"I wouldn't have missed this chance for the world," Bill said, shaking his head as best he could. Terminal cancer had swindled several neck muscles.

"You feelin' okay?"

"Better than ever!"

It was obvious they were more than casual friends. They had an alliance, camaraderie; they were companions. Brian drove us to Cherokee Campground, while Crying Wolf regaled Bill with highlights of the Trail so far, like an excited sailor boy chiming on about his high-sea voyages to his retired captain father.

"Everyday, I've been following along with my maps," Bill said, "pinpointing where I guessed you to be each day, tracing the contours and terrain of the Trail you were going through. I watched you approach Woody Gap. I couldn't wait until you reached Blood Mountain. And then..." He longed again for the Trail himself and lived it vicariously through Crying Wolf.

"Bill, I *wish* you had been there with me," Crying Wolf said.

We arrived at Cherokee Campground and secured our site for the night. Together Bill and Crying Wolf gathered firewood, and I set up my tent. While Bill shaped a masterful fire, I asked Crying Wolf how he knew Bill.

"Brian and I used to work with Bill. Bill is a great woodsman, a survivalist, my mentor, a kindred spirit. Everything I know about the woods, I owe to him. If it weren't for him, I wouldn't be out here."

The atmosphere sighed a tinge of foreboding and remorse, as we watched Bill touch up his neat wooden assembly, ready to light. How much fire was left in Bill? A moment of silence passed, after which Crying Wolf clicked in, "So! This is Bill's own technique. He invented this way to build a fire."

"I hope it works," Bill said.

"He's so modest." Crying Wolf rolled his eyes. "It works every time. Hell, it's foolproof."

"Now that's a fire!" Brian snarled moments later. It was indeed, and we enjoyed ourselves by it, until it was time for Brian and Bill to take Rowdy back home to Atlanta.

"You'll join me, won't you, Bill?" Crying Wolf hoped. "In a couple weeks, if you're feeling OK, that is?"

"You bet!" Bill replied. He always made light of his terminal situation, even when he once confused his medicinal mouthwash in one hand with the cola in the other. His attitude was positive and strong, and I bonded with him from the start.

Crying Wolf made his sad good-byes, petting Rowdy, while I stood aside and watched Bill insert an envelope into Crying Wolf's backpack.

He winked at me, putting his finger to his lips: "Shh…"

I nodded to acknowledge his secret. And they were off.

Crying Wolf sighed.

Descending Rocky Mount the following day, I took the lead. Crying

Wolf seemed melancholy and short on energy.

"I found a letter in my pack from Bill," he said.

I acted unknowingly.

He continued in murmured tones, "He said that if he dies before I finish the Trail—"

I turned to face him, "What?"

"Nothing." And he stopped, turned his head from me to fight a losing battle against his tears. I squeezed his shoulder and he broke down. Crying Wolf palmed his face and said, "Hell, I'm going to miss that guy," and then bowed his head reverently, shedding more tears. That tied knots in my throat, drawing stripes down my own cheeks, but my empathy was only a tint of what he must have felt. The next mile was painful, knowing that Crying Wolf was sprinkling the ground behind me with tears.

One evening spent with Bill left a lasting impression on me. I will remember how his dignity and neighborliness never neglected his failing body and friendship with others. It was no small wonder why Bill's passing would be so difficult for Crying Wolf. It was clear why he was setting one healthy foot in front of the other. Crying Wolf was hiking the Trail for Bill.

Trail Tidbit #7
Larger Than Life

Small World... Small World...
I dreamed... about Earth, my home, while zipping around the Milky Way. I flipped a switch, and my rocket blasted toward c-squared. Pluto. Neptune. Uranus. Saturn. Jupiter. Mars. Earth.

Small World... Small World... I couldn't get the thought out of my head.

"Yeah, it sure is a small world," I said to myself, turning off the light-speed switch. I drifted through space. "Look at her."

Earth. North American continent. Ah... right where I'd left it.

"I think I'll land there, in the middle of nowhere, in the southern area."

My ship's landing gears hummed, and the portal slid open. I sneaked out onto the land and moseyed into a lush forest. A breeze whistled through the treetops.

Small World... Small World...

"Huh?" I cocked my ear up.

Small World... Now I was hearing voices whispering *Small World*.

"Who is that?" I looked behind me. "Who's saying that?!"

Small World... it whispered.

I woke up with a gasp. "Where am I?"

On the Appalachian Trail, in the middle of nowhere.

"Oh, yes." I had been dreaming. The universe. Earth.

The wind whispered in the treetops, *Sssmaaaaaaall Wwwooooorld…*

"Whoa!" I said, rapt by the uncanny sound.

Small World…

There was no one with me. Just the woods. Trees.

Small World…

That tree there. The big one. It seemed to speak to me.

I bumbled over to the tree and stared at it. *Did it just say my name?* I looked left and right to make sure no one was watching and said, "But you're a tree!"

You could call me that. And what are you?

The breezy voice sent chills buzzing up to my hairline, tingling my ears.

"I'm a hiker," I said.

I see. Is that all?

"Of course not," I said. "I'm Small World. I'm Aaron."

The tree shook its branches. *You're telling me* who *you are called. I asked what* you are.

"What are you talking about?" I asked.

Who *is vague. No one but you knows much about you by a name. "I am Aaron" tells me nothing about you. It only tells me how you answer to someone's call.*

"Whoa! Hold a sec," I said. I surveyed the region again to make sure I wasn't making a spectacle out of myself. I didn't usually talk to trees. "Why am I talking to a tree?" I wondered aloud. I yanked on the tree's lowest branch. "Why are you talking to me?"

The tree answered, *Why are you listening to me? You once told me that you wanted out of your box. The best place to begin climbing out is in your mind, so I thought I'd suggest some ideas. May I continue?*

"Uh, sure."

Don't human minds often imagine themselves to be more than they are, and forget (or never discover) what they really are?

"All right, already," I said. "I'm a human. Does that satisfy you?"

Only as much as calling me a tree satisfies me, which is little, the tree answered.

"Okay. A maple tree. How's that?"

The tree seemed to smile. *Calling me a maple tree only classifies my features, just as calling you a Caucasian classifies yours,* said the tree. *Your species finds it urgent to classify everything. And that becomes all you know about it and yourselves.*

"So, Negroid, Mongoloid, or Caucasian only describes our features," I said.

Generally, yes. And "maple" only describes mine, the tree said.

"But something doesn't make sense to me."

What's that?

"If humans classify everything, then we've also classified you as a tree under the plant kingdom."

You catch on quickly, said the tree.

"So, you're implying that you're not just a tree."

More to my point, said the tree, *I'm questioning whether we're more than we think.*

I blurted, "What? Okay, wait a minute. Now you've lost me."

The tree's branches eased up, as if to settle into a more comfortable position. *Fine. Do you think that calling me a maple tree sums up everything about me? What is my "treeness?" What am I beyond the root level? Look at what it means to be human. What IS a human?*

"Interesting," I said. "What *is* a human being really? I mean, any answers given to that question would probably not be universally accepted. Although, I think we could come to a consensus on what features all humans share..."

And are you something more—beyond what you call human? I am called a tree, but I was germinated once, too. Dig under my roots. Dig under your roots and pull up what you see.

"Oh, boy," I sighed and plopped down in the grass. "You mean before I was born?"

The tree answered, *Sure. Think of that sentence: "...before I was born." What is the "I" that was conceived and born?*

I shook my head. "I don't understand."

Have you ever slept in someone else's home? the tree asked.

"Yes."

Tell me about it, said the tree. *Keep it simple.*

"Well, I was visiting a good friend out of town. We chatted until late. She led me to the guest room, and I fell asleep."

Your friend brought you to your room? asked the tree.

"That's right. I was shown where it was."

Where were you before you were shown?

I hesitated, trying to see the tree's point. "Uh, in the living room."

Think of this sentence: "I was in the living room before I was shown to the guest room." In that sentence, what does the "I" refer to? the tree quizzed.

"Me. My body, naturally," I said.

So, your body existed before you were shown to the guest room? asked the tree.

"Don't be silly," I said. "Of course it did."

Then, did your body exist before you were shown into this world—that is, before you were born?

"No, my body did not exist before I was born," I answered.

Okay. Then what does "I" refer to when you say "I was born"?

"Obviously not my body," I said.

Of course not. Then what is "I"?

I scratched my head. "I don't know. I've never thought about it before. I guess I don't get the difference between me and my body." I stretched out and laid my head on my backpack. "All I think I know is that my body didn't exist."

The tree seemed to chuckle.

I saw the humor. "That sounds funny now—'my body,'" I said. "It's like referring to my body as if it were outside of me, like *my* hat, *my* backpack, or *my* boot... *my* body."

Strange, huh? So you weren't born—your body was. And 'Aaron' is what you came to be called after you entered this Room."

"I never thought of things this way. If this body is a belonging of mine, like my backpack, and 'I' am separate from it, then it seems like 'I' exists outside of it."

Maybe. And it seems that you are not separate from your body; it is one with you. And your body will decay—"

"Bringing me back to the state of 'I!'" I howled, pressing my palms into my eyes. "Oh, good Lord!"

Please. The tree seemed to blush. *Just call me Tree.*

"Wait a minute," I said, popping my head out of my hands. "Why does 'I' have to be anything at all?"

What do you mean? asked Tree.

I sighed. "Language is limited. Perhaps we've had no reason to say 'I was born' any differently than we do. It conveys the point we're looking for. Maybe we're being too analytical."

What are you skeptical of? asked Tree. *If you believe in an afterlife, then you can believe in your existence before your body was born.*

My eyelids clapped. "I'm not sure *what* I believe anymore. Afterlife, eternity, God, I just don't know. Who am I? What am I? Who is God, what is God? I just don't know... I just don't know..."

A breeze whispered *Shh,* lulling me to sleep, quenching my thirst for rest.

Trail Tidbit #8
Beware the Bear

Whether you want to hike with comfort or camp in luxury, the weight is on your own shoulders to decide. There are people with over-bloated bundles on their backs, as well as ultra-light backpackers. Most hikers transfer their heavy burdens to the lighter end of the spectrum after a couple weeks, however. An ultra-light pack hangs under twenty-five pounds *with* food and water. For the ultra-lightist it becomes an obsession to drop weight by trading items for their lighter versions or resisting them altogether.

My most memorable ultra-lightist was a soft-voiced man who went by the name Bear. He owned a homemade pack holding only what was necessary for his survival—the "Bear Essentials." Chugging my way up Tray Mountain, I met him overlooking a vista.

"May I join you?" I asked, sitting on a neighboring rock.

Bear took a deep breath. "I've been backpacking all my life…" He took another breath three minutes and several run-on sentences later. Crying Wolf's arrival edited in a period and paragraph mark.

Bear continued, "True thru-hikers only wear sneakers." He stretched out his legs to reveal a qualifying pair. "Yup, they're the only way to go long distance hiking. See, I've been backpacking all my life…"

I clammed up. *True thru-hikers don't do* anything *but hike* through, *from one terminus to the other,* I thought.

Who cared if Bear bore a super light pack and had no tent, but a tarp? He had a hundred bug bites to prove that. What's the point of denying oneself "luxuries" if it adds unreasonable discomfort? I decided to give him the luxury of my absence and moved onward.

Crying Wolf caught up with me on the downside of the mountain, and we settled our tents into place and cooked dinner between them by orange evening sunlight. Bear meandered down the Trail and over to us. He unpacked his food, Whisperlite stove, and fuel bottle.

"Hmph! I'm out of fuel," he said, shaking the container.

"You're out of fuel?"

"Yeah, I dumped it out before making the grueling hike up Tray Mountain," he explained.

"Why?" I asked, as Crying Wolf tossed him his fuel bottle to share.

"Oh, I didn't need to carry the extra weight. That's okay... it was only, what, half an ounce, anyway."

"Half an ounce?!" Crying Wolf choked on a mouthful of rice and beans. "You couldn't carry half an ounce over the mountain?"

I looked up from my pot of noodles at Crying Wolf, who rolled his eyes; his thoughts clearly as cynical as mine: *Yeah, I've been backpacking all my life...*

Crying Wolf and I drank our hot drinks and ate our warm meals. Bear stirred something in his pot for twenty chatty minutes.

"What are you doing?" I wondered aloud.

Bear replied, "Well, I'm trying to cook these split peas. I'm on my emergency rations."

Crying Wolf jerked his head up. "Weren't you just in Helen for two days? And you came out with neither fuel nor food?"

Bears peas bubbled on.

Crying Wolf and I reached Bly Gap two days later. We pitched camp down the hill from the famous Sacred Oak, a gnarled photogenic tree, which marked the entrance into North Carolina—our first state line. The peaceful evening supper suddenly shifted tone.

"Oh, no," muttered Crying Wolf, "Don't move."

"What?" I said, not moving.

"I thought we had lost him for good," Crying Wolf whispered.

It was the incorrigible Bear.

"Crying Wolf, my man!" Bear hollered, noticing our whereabouts.

"Oh, shit!" was written all over Crying Wolf's face.

"You mind if I settle down right here next to y'all?" Bear asked, crashing down between us. Dinnertime filled our stomachs and our ears as Bear babbled on, like his boiling peas. Getting a word in edgewise was like pitching a baseball at him: it either whooshed over his head, unheard, or was batted away, refuted... as if he'd been batting "all his life," or something.

After supper I noticed for the second time that Bear didn't pack out his trash. Instead, he burned it, stamping out his smoldering garbage with the blunt end of his hiking stick.

"Not much into 'pack it in, pack it out,' eh?" I said as politely as I could.

Bear retorted, "Sure I am, but this is paper." It was his wax-coated cardboard container from dinner, with food residue still in it.

"I'm not sure that's low-impact camping, though," I said, as charred leaves glowed around their edges.

"You'll have to explain that one to me," he snapped. "It's *paper*, so it's low-impact."

I didn't like the burnt remains and food residue next to my tent and I didn't want to take the chance of critters and creatures invading our camp because they thought we'd cooked dinner for them. But it was no use. *He'd* backpacked all his life—told me so—and was ticked at me.

We didn't hit it off well from the first inning. He just needed room to be himself, to play the field by himself—the whole field. I had to learn to be more accepting and make some space between us, lots of space. It may be a small world, but a mile or two each day would be fine with me.

Ultra-light, huh? Let me lighten your load, buddy, I thought. *I'll get off your back.*

Trail Tidbit #9
Basic Instincts

ometimes emotions got knocked off track for no clear reason. Gloom pulled me down the other side of Standing Indian Mountain two weeks into the Trail. I felt like a party balloon, whose string had been snipped. Now I was floating away from all the other balloons, alone. *If only I could deflate and come back down to be with the others,* I thought. *Then again, maybe I should be alone for a while.* But I was afraid of losing Crying Wolf. It was possible to be half a day behind someone and never see him again. *Where was Lady Kat, anyway?*

Crying Wolf kindled some chitchat around a fire with new faces, Pathfinder and Archon.

"Sorry I'm not much on words tonight," I said. "Guess I'm a bit tired. G'night."

The next morning, when I told Crying Wolf I was still in a quiet mood, he said, "You might just need some solitude."

I heeded his advice. My day began fighting silly battles with petty irritations. With every step, my pack squeaked in the strap joints. I stopped to adjust it, but it persisted like an unoiled ceiling fan: *squeak, squeak, squeak.* I re-laced the straps, then saddled it onto my back again and took a step forward.

Squeakie. Halting, I grit my teeth. Another couple steps forward...

Squeakie, squeakie! I clenched my fists, disgusted, and took another cautious step forward, as if crossing a busy street.

SQUEAK! Enough! My hands and face wrung together, gouging out a curse. I whipped my arms back, hurled my pack onto the ground and glared at it.

You seem upset.

It was that tree again. I ignored it and paced about.

Why the hullabaloo over a measly squeak? Tree asked.

I had no answer. I felt childish.

It's okay. Take a deep breath. Good. Now have courage to accept what you cannot change, and move on.

My eyes suddenly opened up to the ambient green hue shed by the spring forest. Mosses and lichens gift-wrapped everything. The woody silence melted the ice cap I was wearing. It dribbled down my cheeks, and puddled into a warm song in my throat. The birds sang with me. The all-natural high wooed me from my grief, and I forgot about my squeaking pack straps.

Crying Wolf was right. I had needed some time alone with Mother Nature. He knew that "Mother knows best" how to remedy what ailed me. Yet, all along, I *knew* solitude was what I lacked; time alone to think and listen to the earth. But tending to my own intuitions took awareness of their existence, patience to listen to and understand them, and confidence to act upon them.

That evening yielded rain, which dropped through holes in the night sky and into the crack of dawn. I lay dry in my tent, waiting for the rain to let up. The dense fog and heavy drizzle didn't promise a dry day, however. Its dreariness muffled me. I loathed hiking in the cold rain, and debated returning to the highway at Winding Stair Gap, just over a mile back, which could take me to Franklin, North Carolina.

Go get warm and dry, Small World.

It was Tree.

I peeked out from under my rainfly. "How can you stand the rain, Tree?" I asked.

Can't live without it, Tree answered. *Go get a hot shower and a clean bed.*

"No," I said. "A motel will cost money."

I know money doesn't grow on trees, but trust me. You'll be fine.

"But I've never hitchhiked before. Franklin is ten miles away," I said.

You need a break.

"But I'll lose time."

What's the rush? Tree answered.

"No, I'll overcome this rain," I said.

With my nose toward the ground for four miles, I trudged forward until I reached a shelter. Mileage had amounted to little, but I was wet, chilled, and miserable, so I considered staying. I hem-hawed around, chewing on the idea to return to Franklin. All morning long I'd felt like I was making a mistake. My gut had tried to convince me to repent with every step.

"I can't wimp out because of lousy weather," I said.

Being wet and low in spirits is not wise in cold weather, Tree replied.

"But I'd have to backtrack several miles!" I said.

In the long scheme of things, those few miles are nothing.

"That's true." Tree was right. I could have kicked myself for not having listened to my gut-instincts first thing in the morning. The town of Franklin mocked me from afar, "Wimp! Boohoo!"

I bucked up, set my brow, and backtracked to Franklin despite the constant scorning.

"How do you think you're going to get to Maine," Franklin jeered, "if you can't even suffer a day of rain?"

"You wanna know the truth?" I asked.

"You can't handle the truth! You're so feeble-minded!"

"Franklin, my dear… I don't give a damn!"

Franklin gave up a cozy room, a hot shower, and a rejuvenating meal. I'd be a new man on the morrow: dry, clean, refocused, and a touch more self-assured to listen to what my instincts told me to do.

Trail Tidbit #10

Hot Pursuit

Journal Entry

4/16/00—Just beyond Wayah Bald to Rufus Morgan Shelter (16 miles)

Supply and demand. Demand and supply? Water? Not a chance. Sixteen miles today without a trace of it was an outrage! Who charted this section? Who's responsible for this disaster? Had there been one lot to park my feet in, where water was available, I would have punched out sooner today. Mile after mile, meter after meter, foot after throbbing foot, I pressed onward, looking for something to drink. I thought I was going to tumble down the slope unconscious.

"Come on! Just a little farther," I pleaded with myself. "You can do it."

I sucked the air for moisture.

"You *have* to do it," I said. "There's no place on this ridge to set a tent down."

My ankles howled.

"Where's the stupid shelter, dammit?!"

But some sort of trail-magic came over me (as has been happening more and more often in despairing times). I vanished. *Poof!* I was transported to a new realm of beauty and painless bliss. This was no illusion. A dazzling stream of purple and white flowers trickled alongside the Trail. I gasped in a hushed *Wow!* Enchanting. A fat yellow-striped centipede wriggled on the Trail. I ogled it for several moments.

Poof! Then my eyes spotted two woodpeckers soaring through the leafless trees. My position above caught an unusual sight of flight: the tops of their wings in motion. Birds were always *above* me in the Midwest. Holding still as tapestries, my senses awoke and revealed black squirrels frolicking about in search of acorns, and unseen critters rustling in the fallen leaves. Spellbound, my ears divided my attention onto a couple prancing deer. But there was something out of place.

What was it?

I looked around.

I couldn't see it, but my ears told me that something was not right. Something was out of place.

It was a huffing and puffing sound.

Something was, yes, I heard it again… *panting.*

Like a dog!

But out here in the middle of nowhere?

Neither woodpeckers, nor squirrels, nor deer pant like a dog, as far as I knew. Louder and louder it became until finally the answer darted into view. *Poof!*

"Pant-apant-apant!" huffed a small white dog, hounding the deer in hot pursuit. No doubt this was a domestic animal—and not a hunting breed.

Was it lost?

Was its owner nearby?

I detected no human in the vicinity (other than yours truly).

It was a comedy show for an audience of one—out in the boonies. Better than IMAX, this 3-D panoramic act ended as the deer exited stage right with one carefree pooch hot on their tails.

Then, as if by other wizardry, the barren trees bloomed their emerald hands to greet me as I dropped in altitude. I smiled in return, grateful to see green again. The fairy dust began to fade, just as the shelter appeared… *poof!*

My spirits had come up, and three ibuprofens went down with water from the neighboring creek. I now feel as dilapidated as the shelter I'm writing in. It should be condemned, although it feels like Heaven after my longest hike to date: sixteen miles (on the 16th—a coincidence? *Poof!*) Normally, I prefer my tent to the shelters, simply because it's more comfy, cozy, and private. But I'm too pooped to pitch the tent tonight.

Except for the resident mice, I am alone. Sleep will be sound, even through the wild chanting and scuffling around me. Funky chirps and coos of all sorts fill the full-moonlit night. The grouse batting their breasts with their wings sound like an old John Deere engine. Someone's dog is gnawing on its squeaky toy… either that, or some other animal wheezes like one. I enjoy those noises… but the mice! Every three words I write: *rustle, rustle. Gasp!* Are they into my food? *Rustle, rustle. Gasp!* Are they chewing a hole in my pack? *Rustle, rustle. Gasp!* What if they jump on my face while I sleep? It ruffles my feathers, but it's still good to be here, feeling so victorious about the day's accomplishment.

Trail Tidbit #11
Salad Mountain

Stecoah Gap, in North Carolina, found me dragging my feet, as if I were slogging boulders behind myself. Water was scarce again, and I was running on empty. At the gap, Recycled Teenagers told me of a reliable spring .3 mile off the Trail. *Why couldn't water be nearby?* Thirsty, hungry, and cranky as I dragged my heels to the spring, I left my pack under Recycled Teenagers' care. They were a kind couple. Mr. Recycled Teenager, 71, was thru-hiking for a second time; this round with his wife, 65, who had two titanium knees. Their courage put my crankiness to rest.

When I returned, Lady Kat was taking a breather with Crying Wolf. Back together again! He took her water containers to the spring, and I gave her some company until his return. We pressed through our exhaustion in order to hit the next shelter before sundown. Following Stecoah Gap was an impossibly steep ascent, for which we were not prepared.

"Oh, come on!" we bellowed.

"That's not fair! These trail-maintainers don't have a clue how to build good paths!"

Somehow Crying Wolf scaled that good-for-nothing heap of dirt as if his feet were on fire, while Lady Kat and I lagged behind and whined about it with each baby step.

"Didn't anyone teach these guys about switchbacks?"

We were weary, and the dismal weather wasn't a plus. I was about to grumble about that, too, when Lady Kat turned to me with a gleaming smile.

"Guess what I've got?"

It had better be good, I thought.

Her grin was enough to pull me out of my slump, but her secret was sufficient to haul me up the mountain. She reached inside her waist pouch and snatched out a Snickers candy bar.

"You want half?" she said seductively.

How could I ever repay her! It's a hiker's favorite candy companion—bar none. Snickers really satisfies… to a point.

The sugar fix obliged our energy needs for a bit but not our appetites. Nigh on dinnertime, my cravings for real food kicked in.

"Don't get me wrong, the Snickers was great," I said, "but ya know what I could go for now? A salad!"

Just the thought of fresh veggies stopped us in our tracks, like deer in a speeding truck's headlights.

Lady Kat sighed dreamily.

One lead foot at a time, we persisted to stagger upward, but our minds began to coast.

"Mmm. This is a gigantic mound of rich green lettuce we're climbing," Lady Kat said.

"And look there," I replied, pointing at some trees. "Carrot sticks and broccoli!"

She continued, waving at some lichen-covered boulders, "Oh, do you see those cucumbers? And aren't those green peppers?"

The entire mountain became a luscious salad. Surely we were out to lunch. When a body needs real food, I must say, Snickers doesn't gratify.

"I bet there's a big red cherry tomato on top!" I added.

"Let's go find out!"

There was no tomato. And Brown Fork Gap Shelter had nothing but a plateful of smelly hikers. The next day we'd find a salad in Fontana Village to prepare us for the Great Smokies. That night, however, we had to settle for a kettle of Mac-n-cheese.

Sleepless Smoky Nights

No one breathes. I am startled fully awake as the chain-link fence across the shelter shakes. Something out there wants inside. In the thick of the night, I know it can't be a hiker coming in late.

The fence rattles again.

Wide eyed, only blackness is distinguishable.

Or is that a bear I see?

The air in my throat puddles into my lungs.

No one budges as the chain links jangle again.

Is the fencing really bear-proof?

Adrenaline races through my veins.

My heart crouches into pounce position.

Silence.

I brace myself gingerly onto my elbow.

Where's my knife?

Yet another hushed moment.

Rattle, rattle!

Oh, man! Wild boars!

We'll all be shredded into hog-slop within seconds!

Please, God, no!

My eyes poke around for something to focus on.

I gasp for one final breath and…

Crickets chirp…

God?

Is it gone?

Cheep-cheep, cheep-cheep…

The entire shelter shuffles as every last one of us scrambles for his flashlight, as if on cue.

Flick, click, clack, click…

Nothing there.

The spook had vanished, having lost its appetite for cowardly lions. There is no telling what had crept on the other side; it is gone.

Sleep isn't possible right away. I don't dare count sheep… what if wolves are out there?

I fall asleep….

The following night's slumber at Siler's Bald shelter begins like feathers drifting to the earth. Snuggled deep within my mummy-bag, I straddle the threshold of sleep, where arms and legs deal that final twitch to shake off the day's tension. *Ah…*

Bow-wow-row!

This time I'm jolted awake by barking dogs.

Dogs?

Dogs aren't allowed in the Park!

The Great Smoky Mountains National Park forbids dogs, and requires hikers to use the shelters for protection. Nevertheless, the shelter is full; so, many other hikers are sleeping outside.

Rolf-rolf-rolf!

Wait a minute… those are the manliest dogs I've ever heard!

My sluggish senses snap the pieces together: *Some of the men tenting outside got spooked by something they heard prowling about in the woods and began barking to scare it off.*

"It can't be bears, because bears don't travel in groups," I hear them whisper.

They bark again (still a bone-chilling noise), shining their flashlights in the direction of the rustling footsteps.

"Deer?" they continue. "No, because the eyes are too low to the ground. It could be wild boars."

I fall asleep….

...

The monsters had been scared off, as well as we poor souls in the safeguarded shelter. Everyone was still alive by sun-up. One tenter, Latestart, had been either too lazy or too scared to get out of his tent to pee. I didn't blame him. Among his resources, a Ziplock baggy was made suitable. First thing that morning, a voice rang out from a particular tent, "Oh, crap! My Ziplock leaked!"

No one held his breath. Everyone started laughing until the chain link fence across the shelter shook. Something *inside* had wanted out. Live and learn.

Above: Papa Doc, Lady Kat and I crossed Fontana Dam—the largest dam this side of the Mississippi (480 feet high), built in the early 1940s. On the other side of the dam is the entrance to the Great Smoky Mountains National Park. A chemist, Papa Doc taught me that ascorbic acid (in vitamin C tablets) would neutralize the taste in his water from iodine tablets, which were used for purifying.

Below: At Derrick Knob shelter, hikers hung their food bags in the trees to keep them out of bears' reaches. There wasn't enough room for all of us to sleep in the shelter, so some chanced it in their tents. Land Turtle, Latestart, Nomad, Smilin' Dave were there, as well as a nameless few.

Existential Crisis

The Smokies flourish with more varieties of plants than in all of Europe. That's what was printed on the plaque at Newfound Gap. Trees, trees, and more trees. Hundreds. Thousands. Millions of them crowded the hillsides.

"How many board feet of lumber do you think are in that valley?"

Board feet? my mind screamed, peeking around neighboring tourists to see who'd made the remark. My skin flushed with outrage as he pointed at every tree and named a dollar value.

"After so many years in the lumber industry, all I see is amounts of board feet per tree."

If ears could gag, mine would have vomited. What a sad life. What a stupid industry. Trees have so much to give, so much to say. Being a tree would be enviable. I moved away from the sickening man and picked up my gaze again. *If I were a tree,* I thought, *what stimulating dialogue would I have with the others?*

I scooped up my mind and chucked it into the valley of trees and imagined mingling with all my neighbors. Funny thing was, we all were saying the same things—in different ways, but the same nonetheless. My soundless voice was like a warm, soothing energy—the kind you might feel when you get the nod of approval from a king.

Of course, we trees were speaking not so much to each other, as to the raccoons, birds, mosses, bugs, and other living things. I was telling a squirrel about a perfect notch in my boughs for a nest, when a young man with a backpack hiked up to me, mumbling something about Humanness and Existence. *Oh, yes. That gets them every time,* I thought.

Still hung up on the What & Who questions, are you, Small World? I said.

"Oh, hello Tree," he said. "Yes, I see how Who is vague, but *what* presents a problem for me, too."

How so? I asked.

"The word *what* implies a noun—a thing. All that exists is a thing, or it wouldn't exist," he said.

Seems logical, I said.

The hiker continued, "I grew up learning that all *things* were created by God, and that God is eternal and uncreated." He paused.

I said nothing but waved a branch as if to say, "Go on."

"If everything exists as a thing that was created by God, then what about God?" he asked.

Ah, the age-old "Where did God come from?" question, I said. *You told me you were taught that God is eternal and uncreated.*

"That's what they told me. But then God is not a thing, because he created all things, according to the doctrine. Therefore, if God is no thing... he is nothing!"

Are you concluding that God does not exist? I asked.

"Now I don't know if God exists, or not. I just feel as if there's something illogical about the doctrine I grew up with."

Kierkegaard said, "God does not exist. He is eternal." Perhaps God is beyond anything we can imagine or comprehend, I said.

"Maybe he is. Unimaginable, incomprehensible, unknowable. But that still doesn't prove anything. And don't tell me it's all about having faith. That's fickle to me. I want evidence!"

Small World, look at your body. Look at the dirt, the grass, the trees, the whole earth, sky, stars, and universe...

He thought he saw where I was going with this. "Ah, the age-old 'It-all-had-to-come-from-somewhere' argument," he said. "Isn't it possible that everything always existed; that all matter is eternal? That would mean that God did not create it."

I replied, *If everything is eternal, then that would leave open the possibility that God is also an eternal thing...*

"…And therefore would exist," Small World added. "A possibility. Now this leads me to a new question."

Go ahead.

"Evidence shows us that the earth wasn't always here as we know it. Scientists say it's only five billion years old, and the universe is about 13 billion years old. And new stars are being born all the time. But if matter is eternal, then what was the universe before it was born 13 billion years ago?"

I was silent for a few moments, allowing the human time to think about his question. Then I said, *You seem to be implying that matter has always existed in one form or another—if not as a complete universe, then as something else.*

"That's right," he answered.

I continued, *You have your wise men who say that all matter is simply condensed energy.*

"Einstein, I believe," he said. "Yes. Energy is the basis for all matter."

If you were the size of an atom, you could pass through my tree trunk in a straight line without hitting another atom. But what about atoms? Are they not also forms of energy? If the atoms of the universe are simply energy, then the real question is What is energy?

"Everything is energy," he said.

Therefore, everything is One, I said.

"Uh-oh."

What now?

"Does this mean that energy is, or is not, a *thing*?" he asked.

You're going to have me here all day, aren't you? I laughed. *Next, you'll ask me where energy comes from. Some say that energy is the residue of absolute wisdom and knowledge.*

Small World squeezed his head between his fists. "Oh, God!" he yelled. "God, oh, God!"

God, perhaps, I said. *Makes ya wonder, how it's all connected though, huh?*

Top Left: Snow! I was surprised how hot I felt after 15 minutes of hiking, when there was three inches of the fluff on the ground.

Top Right: The day after snow was hot!

Bottom: Papa Doc toasted himself at Brown Fork Gap.

Trail Tidbit #14
The Show Must Go On

APRIL 28, 2000. THE GREAT SMOKY MOUNTAINS

Silence. At daybreak a small, three-sided stone hut is seen on a mountainside. A wooden sign on the wall is engraved: Peck's Corner Shelter. Light puffs of smoke sail around its chimney. Inside the shelter sleep seven hikers—seven lumps of mummy-bags. Backpacks hang on the walls.

A rosy face pokes out of a blue sleeping-bag, looking up at her frozen breath. She, WACKY JACKIE, sits up, and her face widens as she's shocked by something she sees outside. She's speechless—because of the sight, and because other hikers are still asleep. With a woolen hand, she stirs awake her partner, WALKIN' HOME. WALKIN' HOME's nose pokes out of his bag. WACKY JACKIE taps him again. He sits up, and uncovers his head, as she points a mitten outside the shelter. He gasps at what he sees. Soon six more faces rouse from the other sacks.

LADY KAT
  Snow!

PAPA DOC
> Unbelievable!

SMALL WORLD
> There's gotta be at least three inches of it out there.

WALKIN' HOME
(flopping back onto his sleeping pad)
> Do I have to get up?

      Everyone scrambles out of his sack. PAPA DOC stokes the smoldering embers in the fireplace. Then in unison they roll up their sleeping-bags.

BEAN
> God, I feel like the Seven Dwarfs.

SMALL WORLD
(singing)
> Roll it! Stuff it! Pack it!

WALKIN' HOME
> Need calories to produce heat, folks. Might wanna get your stoves.

SMALL WORLD
(singing)
> Prime it! Light it! Boil it!

LADY KAT
(giggling but sarcastic)
> Thank you, Small World.

      While stoves are lit and water begins to boil, hikers stand around them, rubbing their hands together near the small flames. Others have their arms crossed, buffing their shoulders. BEAN unwraps a Pop-Tart.

PAPA DOC
(rich Maine accent)
> Boy, is it nippy! People have become hypothermic in as much as 56 degrees Fahrenheit.

CHRIS

It's a bit nippier than that, Doc. Irish whiskey, anyone?

WACKY JACKIE

I think I had enough of that last night.

SMALL WORLD

I'll take a swig! Goes good with oatmeal.

CHRIS hands SMALL WORLD the bottle, while the other hikers shove oatmeal and Pop-Tarts into their mouths, dancing in place.

SMALL WORLD
(singing)

Eat up! Drink up! Clean up! Pack up! Let's go!

LADY KAT

Small World's drunk.

PAPA DOC

If we're the Seven Dwarfs, Small World, you must be Dopey.

Laughter.

LADY KAT

I gotta get moving, I'm freezing. I'm sure you'll catch up to me.

The scene closes with six frenetic people finishing packing up.

ONE HOUR LATER

Every tree wears costumes of ice and snow, which slink off its limbs when the wind whistles. A lone hiker inches forward through the snow-covered Trail. It's LADY KAT, hunched over with an arm across her forehead. SMALL WORLD enters the scene, staggering 25 yards behind her.

SMALL WORLD
(hollering)

Lady Kat!

The howling wind waters down his voice, shaking sheaths of ice from the treetops. SMALL WORLD is pummeled by them. He shields his face and tightens the cord of his hat under his chin.

SMALL WORLD
(hollering)
> Lady Kat!

LADY KAT rears around, squashing her hat to her pelted head.

LADY KAT
(laughing, screaming)
> Help! Small World!

The wind picks itself up and throws it against the landscape again. The view over the valley whitens, and the trees blur as snow whips around them.

SMALL WORLD
(yelling)
> Look out! Here it comes!

SMALL WORLD and LADY KAT huddle together as ice crashes on their heads, hands, and packs. Nose to nose, they ad-lib hysterical laughs and exclamations.

LADY KAT
> It's like ice-nettles—it stings!

SMALL WORLD
> Can't stop for long, Lady Kat. Gotta keep warm. Let's just get to the next shelter.

LADY KAT
> Yes! It's only 5.2 miles from Pecks Corner shelter.

SMALL WORLD
> Thank God! That's not far, but in this weather....
> *Side by side, they pace their steps equally, crunching through snow and ice until they arrive at the next shelter. LADY KAT and SMALL WORLD throw off their backpacks and hustle to snap camp together.*

LADY KAT
(singing)
> Unpack it! Unstuff it! Unroll it!

SMALL WORLD
(joining in, singing)
> Warm up! Dry up! Cheer up!

> *Minutes later, PAPA DOC chugs up to the shelter, red and shivering. LADY KAT reaches a pot of boiling hot chocolate over to him.*

SMALL WORLD
> Some weather, eh?!

PAPA DOC
> Some birthday present, I'll say.

LADY KAT
> Well, happy birthday, Papa Doc! Which one is it?

PAPA DOC
> Sixty-eighth.

SMALL WORLD
> Here, have a Snickers bar. Happy Birthday!

> *The scene closes as dinner has been eaten, and a shelter is full of hikers curled up in their sacks. PAPA DOC munches on a Snickers candy bar. Night falls.*

APRIL 29, 2000. TRI-CORNER KNOB SHELTER

> *Silence. The morning sun lights the inside of a shelter, littered with backpacks, boots, cooking gear, and a dozen sleeping hikers. One of them stirs and stretches, another turns over, and several begin to rouse. WALKIN' HOME props himself up on his elbow. He cocks his head with a perplexed brow as he looks outside.*

WALKIN' HOME
(whispering)
> Pst! Wacky Jackie, wake up.

> *WACKY JACKIE pokes her nose out of her sleeping-bag.*

WALKIN' HOME
(whispering)
> You gotta take a look at this.

> *WACKY JACKIE sits up and uncovers her head as WALKIN' HOME points a hand to look outside the shelter. WACKY JACKIE'S jaw drops.*

WACKY JACKIE
(full voice)
> It's gone! Wow, my thermometer reads about 55 degrees!

> *Everyone else in the shelter rises: sitting up, propping up on elbows, or lifting heads up. SMALL WORLD looks at his thermometer, too, and shakes his head.*

PAPA DOC
> Well, that's spring mountain weather for you!

SEVERAL HOURS LATER

> *The sun has risen to the top of the sky. Rugged mountains, covered in green pines and barren deciduous trees, fold themselves across the land. Within them are tiny people with large packs on their backs, stomping along a pathway.*

> *The scene flashes between points, different hikers in different locations, at different paces: a lone CRYING WOLF; a pair—WALKIN' HOME and WACKY JACKIE; a single BEAN; one PAPA DOC a few paces ahead of LADY KAT; and finally, a solitary SMALL WORLD. His heavy boots march on a muddy trail. His shorts and t-shirt are sweat-drenched under a snug backpack. Swinging from a zipper on his backpack is a plastic thermometer. It reads 70 degrees. He is smiling.*

SMALL WORLD
(to himself)
> Spring Mountain weather. Quick-change comedian.

THE END

Trail Tidbit #15

Weight, I'm On My Weigh!

"Food, glorious food..." the number one topic of fireside chats and hikers' honors.

"When I get to town, I'm eating a stack of pancakes and eggs."

"How'd ya like to have a fat, juicy burger right now?"

Food market dialogues are similar to those of non-hikers.

"How many calories does this have?"

"How much fat is in that?"

But what is *not* heard among non-hiking shoppers is, "Bah! Not enough calories and fat. Put it back!"

Hiking for several hours "in one sitting" was an all-day, everyday StairMaster session, burning 4,000-6,000 calories every time. After a strenuous haul, my titanium pot whipped up large meals of pasta and rehydrated veggies, or rice and beans, or instant mashed potatoes. Homemade jerky and a Snickers bar rounded off a typical supper, quenching my cravings for proteins, salts, and fats. Of course, I popped a vitamin tablet to call it all healthy.

Several weeks northward passed before I really wanted breakfast, though. Some hikers smeared peanut butter on Pop-Tarts, but I ate them plain or stuck to eating oatmeal (no, *I* did not stir chocolate Slim-Fast powder into mine).

Sporadic snack times and lunchtimes answered the plea for help of sluggish legs, serving a bagel with cheese and salami, an energy bar, dried fruit, or a handful of GORP (Good Ol' Raisins and Peanuts—with M&Ms). My biggest appetite was at dinnertime, however, and when the senses sharpened in the Outdoors, sniffing out a cheeseburger's whereabouts in nearby towns was easy as pie.

Mountain Mama's Kuntry Store, known to have a mean grill, sat two miles outside the north exit from the Great Smoky Mountains National Park, twenty miles from any town. The river rushing behind the store was getting louder, and the scent of a veteran grill thickened as Papa Doc and I neared.

The door jingled as we entered, freeing the trapped wafts of cooked grease.

"What'll it be, boys?" asked the big-haired belle behind the counter. She knew we were there for one reason only.

We gave our order, drooling.

"Coming right up," she said, and turned to the cook, "Two cheeseburgers and fries!"

Papa Doc and I waited for our meals at a rickety booth next to the window and stared at all the snacks and knickknacks for sale, stuffed animal heads on the walls, racks of several candy bar brands, an Elvis portrait, Ramen noodles.

"Thank God! Here comes our food," I said.

Papa Doc twisted around in his seat to make sure.

Sure enough. Sitting before us were two of the biggest hamburgers we'd ever seen, dripping with cheese and mustard, packed with pickles, lettuce, tomatoes—the works. They tipped the scales of Appalachian Excellence. I drowned my fries in ketchup and wrapped my mouth around a handful of sandwich.

"Oh! Mmm. Dis is absowutwy wunnerful!" I said, careful not to spit.

Three bites later, we finished our plates.

"Want some ice cream?" Papa Doc asked.

"Move over Richard Simmons!" I said. "Bring it on!"

Not to worry! The scale next to the freezer of hand-dipped ice cream told me that I'd lost 25 pounds. Jenny Craig would have been proud. Doctor Atkins might have freaked (what, with all those carbs!), but results have shown this Appalachian Diet to work: guaranteed. Such grueling daily grinds burned these foods so quickly, we pack-mules begged for more. I ate like a horse; was dirty as a pig, but worked like a dog!

But waffle cones, chocolate bars, and grills didn't hold a flame to fresh fruits and vegetables. Salad bars were miraculous feeding troughs, plundered every time by us gypsies. Carrying perishables was impractical, due to their shelf life, weight, and price. So, I longed for roughage.

Pounding down a slope, I was stopped by an elderly group of men who were curious about me, drawing from blatant clues that I was a thru-hiker: grubby clothes plus greasy hair plus dirty fingernails equals a smelly thru-hiker... While I paraphrased my story, one gentleman reached into his rucksack, and then spun his wrist around toward me to reveal a shiny golden apple. My jaw unhinged with a sigh of delight, as I accepted this Trail Angel's blessing without hesitation. My gratitude was obvious when I became to that fruit as an emaciated snake in a rat's nest. The poor old men gawked at me as if I was an American at an English tea-party.

Anywhere there's food, there's a hiker, I thought, which reminded me of a joke.

"An M&M was sitting on the ground next to the Trail one day. Suddenly a day-hiker bounced up over the hill, where the M&M was sitting. But the day-hiker strolled on past, ignoring Li'l M. Then a section-hiker drew near and poked at the M&M. And, of course, the section-hiker left the M&M behind in the dust. Next a thru-hiker was seen stomping up the path. The thru-hiker marched straight up to the M&M shouting, "Hallelujah! Look what I've found!" then picked it up... and ate it!"

Did I eat to hike, or hike to eat? All that mattered was finding my way to Maine, one bite at a time. Anything to gain miles, and lose inches was fine with me.

My Dike Overfloweth

Lacing up a sixteen-mile day, my boots settled on the only available flat patch of land. Old logging roads, grassy or not, are one reason why freestanding tents have advantages over my stake-anchored type. Aluminum stakes are impossible to drive into gravel-packed ground. Shifting to several positions, I worked and worked the stakes until my tent stood somewhat upright. There always seemed to be a stubborn rock or root preventing easy setup.

Pestering flies shared the site with me, as well as a father-son duo who were hiking a short southbound section of the Trail. Crossing paths with section hikers reminded me how fleeting life is; they added a sense of purpose and acceptance to wherever I was on my path, and I knew I would never see them again after tonight.

Eric helped me build a fire to smoke out the bugs, while his father, Walter, prepared their meal. Logs ablaze, and my Lipton noodles cooked through, I sat to eat while Walter and his son still squabbled over rice or noodles.

"Fine. Instant Rice it shall be," Walter said. "Now how do I turn on this stove?"

"Isn't there a switch? Lemme see it," Eric replied.

"No, wait. Just gimme a lighter."

"OK, here."

Flick.

"Hm. Nothing."

"Open the gas valve," said Eric.

"Oh. OK. Now what."

"Flick the Bic!"

Poof! Fireball. But the stove was lit.

Virgin hikers, I thought smugly.

I offered some small talk, and Walter asked where I grew up.

"Grand Rapids, Michigan," I replied.

"Oh, are you Dutch?" he asked, familiar with the city's very-Dutch influence.

"No, thank God!" I blurted.

Tardy thoughts quickly took their seats in my mind: "Uh, you're not Dutch... are you?" I asked, feeling a bit of resistance. If words were tent stakes, then that stake didn't stick—Walter was indeed an immigrant from the Netherlands.

Open mouth, insert foot, bite down hard, I thought to myself.

Shifting around, looking for a better place to jab my stake in, I said, "Hoo-boy! That was rather ill timed. *Wooden shoe* agree?"

Okay, now I was choking on my foot. This stake just wasn't going to find a hold. But, like a true camper, I kept trying.

"Well, you know what they say: 'If ya ain't Dutch, ya ain't much!'"

Walter chuckled and told me not to worry about it; he was an American now. Great! I finally stuck the stake. The roof was raised. The ice was broken. I made a mental note to make sure that next time all stakes could be driven in before I even pitched my tent, just to spare myself the humiliation.

Above: Max Patch is a bald. No one knows exactly how balds formed; although some people theorize that these "naked mountaintops" are a result of the Natives' practice of fire ecology, weather or insect damage, overzealous sheep, or emergency landing spots for hill-loving martians' UFOs.

Below: Papa Doc and PA headed to Hot Springs, North Carolina.

Trail Tidbit #17
Devils in Hot Springs

rail Towns, like experienced fishermen, reel in the unwary with ease. Open a tavern door, and a hiker will pounce on the lures: hamburgers, cold beers, good music. Throw in a laundromat and a hotel with a hot shower and you're sure to hook a keeper. These Ponds of Pleasure capitalize on the seasonal spawn of pilgrims, and departing is like swimming upstream. The generosity of Trail Angels (or should I say Trail Anglers?) is impossible to resist. A town's snagging hook may not always be due to angels and pizza, however, but to the mischievous spells of Trail Demons.

At Hot Springs, North Carolina, I loaded my empty rig at The Sunnybank Inn, affectionately known as "Elmer's." Wiped out, I cut the throttle to refuel at this unique guesthouse, the former home of balladist Jane Gentry. All fourteen rooms of the 1875 Victorian house were garnished with relics of its era. Stepping inside was like being siphoned through a time warp. And guests were fed organic vegetarian meals family-style.

Two days later, the Trail mustered my feet to return, but my body couldn't catch up. I decided to relish another day in town, and frugality decided to find a place to pitch my tent. A townsman offered me a quiet plot of land, on which I could safely camp—alone. Crying Wolf was somewhere ahead of me, and Lady

Kat lagged behind. So, the afternoon was spent on the front porch of renowned AT guru "Wingfoot". Several chatty hours later, I returned to my tent for dinner.

I grabbed my fuel bottle and cranked the pump shaft to prime it.

Crack!

"Just great! Save money in a tent, but pay for it by breaking your gear! Good move, Slick!" said the little devil on my left shoulder.

· "Oh, sleep it off. Everything will work out fine. Tomorrow," said the angel on my right.

Nodding off while journaling, I pulled my sleeping-bag over me to cut the chill. *Slosh!* Jolted upright, I flung the soppy sack off with a gasp. Pitiful, helpless, I sat there with a blank stare, unable to decipher how I got myself into this mess. *Neither did I pitch my tent over a spring, nor did I bring water insi—Wait... a prank!* I could only suspect the neighborhood kids... the little devils! *They maliciously bucketed water into my tent while I was away.* I wanted to be angry, but couldn't; wanted to cry, but was unable. *What to do, what to do?* I had to get out and do something... so I located a payphone and called my mom.

"Chalk it up as a bad experience," she said, encouraging me to take charge, to keep going. "Find a room for the night. You need it now."

I hung up the phone knowing there was no room at the Inn. Dark and cold, the night left me wandering the streets.

It's eleven o'clock. The Inn is full, the motel has no vacancies, my tent is soaked... where do I go? What do I do now?

Pacing the neighborhood to keep warm brought me past Wingfoot's place, hoping for help. On the front porch, he was tied up with his cordless phone, so I waved nonchalantly as I passed. He probably figured I was out to enjoy the stars. *What to do, what to do?*

The hammock in Elmer's yard hung an offer to bed down, but the cool air nipped at my damp clothes. I shivered like an unbalanced washing machine, cocooned in bed sheets, which had been hanging out to dry. I longed for daybreak. Morning stirred the stars into a vivid celestial blue bowl, and without hesitation, I whipped up another zero-day to dry my equipment, solve my fuel pump dilemma, and get some now much-needed rest. The local backpacking shop gave me a new pump shaft, free of charge.

Then Lady Kat arrived into town, which was uplifting. She bunked at the Sunnybank Inn.

"Where are you staying tonight?" she asked.

"I'm just tenting on someone's lawn." I explained. "How do you like it here at Elmer's?"

Just then, Elmer peeked into the room where Lady Kat and I were talking.

"Wingfoot called for you," he said to me. "He thought you stayed here again last night."

"Really?" I said. "Do you know why he called?"

"He just wanted to know if you were all right."

My heart was warmed. Simply flustered, I was okay… ready, willing, and able to move on, even if the current was flowing against me.

In spite of fishy business and four days in the net, I flipped out of Hot Springs the next day and landed safely back where I belonged on the Trail. The Appalachian Trail only occasionally emptied into stagnant ponds, but I learned that determined fish could always find an outlet from murky waters.

Above: Misty morning mountainside.

Below: Fenway and (Strong As) Nails took a break in Big Bald shelter before convincing me to "keep what I see."

Trail Tidbit #18
WYSIWYG

Hemmed by trees for days at a time, I longed for broad mountaintop views every now and again. In fact, anything treeless caught my fancy, even in the early North Carolinian days.

"Hey, look!" someone hollered, "A field!"

Lightning quick, everyone gathering water at the creek abandoned his filter and water bottles to take a gander. Indeed, it was a lush green meadow, no trees… stunning.

Big Bald boasted panoramas that were 360 times better than what we'd seen for days, and the skies looked promising when I crawled out of my tent. I bundled together my load and ate breakfast on the run, anticipating the praised hilltop. The higher I climbed, the more intense the winds blustered. The trees offered some protection, but by the time I came out of the woodwork and onto Big Bald, gray clouds had annexed its crest, vetoing vistas. Hat clutched to my head, hiking poles swinging from my wrists, I bowed before the regal winds—my breath cut short by its sharpness.

The Trail was nearly smudged from sight, and I feared getting lost, let alone weather-blown. Scurrying to the other side of the mount wasn't a breeze, especially without my scenery, but I had no choice. Big Bald shelter lay only a mile or so from the peak. When I arrived, I decided to call it a day, and if the weather cleared (which, by golly, it now teased to), I vowed to make a U-turn for a quick sightseeing tour.

While I bunked in the shielding shelter, a couple of hikers—Fenway and Nails—arrived. They were blessed with magnificent views atop Big Bald. *It figures,* I thought.

"Yeah, they were great," Nails confessed, "but that's nothing compared to what's coming!"

"I know, but I was really looking forward to it," I whined. "Now that the weather is clearing up, I think I'm gonna go back. It's not that far away. At least, not in light of the entire Route."

"Why?" she asked. "A friend once taught me a really helpful lesson: 'What you see is what you get.' What you experienced on Big Bald was what *you* got when you were there. That was *your* story. I think you should keep going. Come camp with us tonight!"

Nails was right. I really felt the adventure in what she was saying. What I tasted on Big Bald was chewable—different than the bite they got—but swallow-able nonetheless. I was learning to eat what was served before me with gratitude— always a process for me. So, I broke my former vows and hiked an additional five miles with Fenway and Nails, in beautifully sun-patched forests, strewn with tiny white flowers like confetti on a ball field after a big win.

Crying Wolf's words echoed in my mind: *The mountains will teach you everything you need to know.*

What you see is what you get, the mountain whispered.

"I get it," I said. "It's as if to say, 'Hey, this is me. Take it or leave it.' What you see is what you get."

Be true to yourself.

"Yeah, like Janis Joplin said, 'Don't compromise yourself. You're all you've got'."

Tough as nails, these lessons—to take what I got on the Trail, and to be true to myself—were important for my feeling at home on the Trail, and within myself. My gaze had to be fixed forward. If I put my hand to the plow, and looked back, then maybe I wouldn't have been fit for the journey after all. I chose to plow forward.

Pick a Path

had four legs. Two of them wore boots, *left, right, left, right,* and the others stabbed the ground ahead of me as hiking poles, *right, left, right, left.* I pressed into them to pull me up the hill. They took a lot of heft off my knees and spared me from many face-plants.

You have a unique body.

I never knew how Tree was going to sprout up again. "That's flattering," I said, "coming from a tree."

Can you think of any other animal on Earth that walks upright on two legs? asked Tree.

"What about birds?" I said.

Birds don't count, because their main mode of transportation is flight.

"Not ostriches. Not chickens," I replied.

Tree sighed. *My point is that you're one of a kind. Even primates still walk on their front knuckles. And ostriches and chickens don't walk upright, either.*

"That is odd," I said. "I wonder why that is."

Why is anything the way that it is? asked Tree.

"Well, that depends upon whom you ask," I answered. "Some scientists would say 'Natural Selection,' and religious fundamentalists would say that God created it that way. Others would say both."

One thing we know for sure is that you are here, said Tree.

"I know *that* I am, but I still wonder *what* I am—what 'I' is. If everything is One, because everything is energy, then you and I are One."

In essence, said Tree.

"Oh, great. Now I sound like a New-ager. I'll be branded a heretic," I said.

Tree replied, *You shouldn't be. Think about it. We showed up on Earth. Neither of us had bodies before they were born. Now both of our bodies contain the same elements: carbon, hydrogen, oxygen, etc. If we're made of the same stuff here, how far-fetched is it to think that we are One out there?*

"Makes sense to me," I said.

Yet you're worried about being branded a heretic?

"Well, my upbringing keeps ringing in my ears: 'The Bible says…' If a teaching contradicts the Bible, then it probably isn't true. How can I just ignore that?"

Why ignore anything? The Bible has a lot to say. So do other writings of other cultures.

"Yo, there it goes again in my head. Can all the world's Scriptures be right?"

The point isn't who is right and who is wrong. If truth wants to be understood and received by anyone who wills, then who can say that one particular culture has found none? And who can say that another culture has found it all? In the search for truth, everyone who looks shall find some. The question becomes What truth have they found?

"I don't know what to believe anymore. There are so many ways," I said.

Perhaps it will help you to understand that there is one Way and one Truth, but many different paths to experience them. There is no one right Path to follow. Is there only one right Method to hike to Maine?

"No. Everyone does it differently."

Everyone's journey varies. There is no one right method to reaching Maine, but simply to go forward. For your journey, it may help you simply to move forward, enjoying your Path with an open mind, seeing it from many different viewpoints. Look high. Look low. Look around. Every journeyman has the fire of life in him or her. The Truth is ablaze with this Life. Life is the Way to follow. It's not about being wrong or right, but whether or not you experience Life.

"Okay," I said, "But one view at a time, I say."

Sure. One step at a time. Just keep walking.

Trail Tidbit #20
Getting Hitched

Thumbing lifts into town became a regular chore, although humbling for suburban boys, like myself. My artistic abilities never lent themselves to hitchhiking—I forever found it tricky to master. Whether I was alone or with others, I seemed to have an uncanny knack for jinxing efforts to catch a ride. Usually, someone else's talents had to snare a car.

Lady Kat and I had had dinner in town and needed a ride back to our accommodations at Uncle Johnny's hiker hostel on the outskirts of Erwin, Tennessee. Shaking my head in disbelief at the number of passing cars, despite our waving thumbs, I suggested, "Maybe it's my hat. Should I take it off? Perhaps I look too sinister."

"Couldn't hurt," Lady Kat shrugged.

I removed my wide-brimmed Australian sun-hat. Unsuccessful.

"Maybe your shaggy hair is scaring them away now," she said.

"Okay. You're a woman. Flash your legs out there and entice someone for us!" I said.

A man in a pickup truck pulled over and hollered at us to jump into the cab, the back was full of tools. Lady Kat and I glanced at each other, and she batted her eyes to imply, "Not bad, eh?" I narrowed my eyes, "Just get in." She yanked the door open as the driver cleared space, flipping beer cans behind the seat, some empty, some full. Now batting my eyes to imply, "Nice going, Lady Kat," she narrowed her eyes at me as if to say, "Can it, bucko. I got you a ride, didn't I?"

"Just kick the cans to the side," the man said, pointing to the floor with a half-drunk beer can in his hand, and an unopened one between his legs.

Just kick the can… my thoughts tiptoed, hoping we didn't just make a fatal mistake. Perhaps accepting the ride wasn't one of our more brilliant moves, but we were only two miles from our destination, and our stomachs were too full of pizza. Sure, Lady Kat's feminine pizzazz may have neutralized my jinxing curse just enough to get a hitch, but it didn't guarantee the driver wouldn't be drunk. The man's speech and maneuvering slurred the whole way.

Superstition aside, the larger the hitching group was, the lesser my presence seemed to blight it. Troupes of five performed surprisingly well. Of course, it took some creativity on our part. Five grubby hobos waving, smiling, dancing in sync, and trying to look as obnoxious as tolerable secured rides again and again. Our theory was, "With these charades, we certainly don't look dangerous. It's only a matter of space." And there were plenty of pickup trucks… most of which sped past, causing us to wonder why they were called 'pickup' trucks. Finally, one would stop.

"You all looked so ridiculous, I felt sorry for you!" a driver explained. "Made me think, 'Geez. No one is ever going to pick up five hitchhikers,' so I had to turn back and get you."

Who says obnoxiousness never pays?

If it wasn't others' talents, then it was an act of God that provided my wishes. The Appalachian Trail emptied out next to a grocery store in a small town, where the local Catholic church ordained a fine hostel for pilgrims such as myself. Too far away from the hostel to do any unnecessary walking, I thought that the grocery store parking lot would be the perfect place to shop for a ride.

"Excuse me," I said to a middle-aged lady, "do you know where I might find The Holy Family Hostel & Hospice?"

She checked off a long shopping list of directions. My Trail Companion book contained the ingredients to make the way, but playing dumb often produced fruit. I liked fruit.

"I'm sorry. I'm not from around here… you've lost me," I said in my most polite tone, projecting the thought, *Can you give me a lift?*

"I don't usually pick up hitchhikers, but… I'll trust God today," the lady decided, sizing me up. Exhausted, I was glad this was her day to have faith. Maybe she was ready to do another good deed, because God had just made fresh cookies.

She declined my offering gas money upon arrival, but I let her know how much we thru-hikers appreciated such services.

Overall, hitchhiking was a fantastic experience. Meeting various people who were intrigued by backpackers' endeavors was often mutually inspiring. One lady's son was biking across Australia, another son was backpacking across Europe. Karmic reasoning persuaded many a worried mother: "I just hope someone will be there for my son when he's in need." One way or another, someone eventually would be persuaded to stop. Determination, a stroke of ingenuity, or simple trust in the goodness of at least one person out there, would lift the feat.

Left: The Nolichucky River.

Top Right: Cool Hand Luke had found something to eat in the store at Uncle Johnny's Hiker Hostel in Erwin, Tennessee. Fennel sorted her gear at Uncle Johnny's.

Bottom Right: Over Hump Mountain (another bald), I tip-toed past monsters with horns on their heads. One in particular— obviously a male (a-hem!)—wore jewelry in his nose. With "mountain oysters" that large, it surprised me that he needed to show off flashy paraphernalia.

Trail Tidbit #21
Holy War

Abreakfast sunrise. A midday cascade. A twilight vista. Everyday. In the Spring? Not on your life! Give me such a place, and I would flee from there like a gnat out of Hell, ticked off. The most pestering problem I had throughout the Trail was with bugs.

Swat!

"Papa Doc said that black flies were the *Maine* State Bird," I grumbled.

Swat!

"Well now I know," I continued, "don't count your chiggers before they hatch!"

Handfuls of no-see-ums and black flies swarmed around me like locusts on a cornstalk. I was afraid to breathe, especially through my mouth. I learned to talk through my teeth. Water holes were clouded with nippers, making it tortuous to refill. I wondered how many bug eggs I had pumped through my water filter. But, oh, their bites were the hiker's bane.

Black flies (buffalo gnats) lacerate the skin, and spit an anticoagulant into the hole in your flesh, so it may continue slurping your blood. Chiggers (harvest mites) stab their mouthparts into the skin and squirt a tissue-dissolving juice. They feed off the liquefied flesh.

Was it the black flies or the chiggers that brought me to the brink of madness in Tennessee? Buffalo gnats stampeded me; I reaped truckloads of harvest mites. Relentless itching ravished me to tears and infection. These friggin' bugs would have been the perfect Chinese torture, or the most effective tool for the Inquisition. Let me show you what happens.

Lying in my tent, I was ready for sleep… upon many a night, many an ungodly night. It all would begin with one particular bite wound.

Rub, rub, scratch, scratch, right?

Wrong.

See, scratching got the Swat Team's attention and motivated it to conspire with all the other fly holes and chigger pits to rally around at eleven o'clock and instigate an Itch Fest. The Airforce band played their bagpipes outside my tent. Whimpers of agony whipped around like a frantic wind trapped in my tent, where I writhed and twisted upon my mat. Good Lord, it didn't stop, even after I'd scratched myself bloody. Panic hissed through my spine. Eventually the commander would order, "Cease fire!" and the battle would die down, although two or three smart-alecks always sniggered and teased, until I fell asleep.

As soon as black flies and chiggers went out of season, mosquitoes cropped up, especially during the wet days of summer. A record harvest of rain was collected into standing puddles—a mosquito's breeding grounds. Sabotaged by the flying armies of bloodthirsty critters, I flailed my arms about to shoo them away. Armies under mission don't heed suggestions from the enemy, however, so I donned my armor to withstand their blows and weaken their forces. My headnet and tubes of itch crème were my allies.

It was Armageddon. Great trials and tribulations on every side. Everyone bellowed his war cry and bore his scars—not proudly—with vengeance. Our only weapons were time and DEET. Many soldiers dropped like flies, but some marched on. I marched on… in misery.

> *Mine eyes have seen the glory*
> *of the coming of the hordes:*
> *But we're trampling through the mountains*
> *where their wings of wrath had soared;*
> *We hath loosed the fateful bug-dope,*
> *and now peace is our reward:*
> *The swarms are buzzing off.*
>
> *Glory, glory, hallelujah!*

Trail Tidbit #22
40 Mays and 40 Mights

People from all walks of life attempted to thru-hike, and each had his own idea of what a true thru-hike was. He may have been a Purist—one who only followed every AT blaze without slack-packing. A Slack-packer was a hiker without his backpack (which may have been taken to the next point for him by someone else). Hikers may have been Blue-blazers, who took alternative trails on their walks to Maine (or Georgia). Aqua-blazers canoed the Shenandoah River for a week. And Yellow-blazers rode the pavement for a stretch. (It's agreed, however, that since they were not actually self-propelled, it wasn't fair to call them "thru-hikers"). A veteran hiker remarked, "Golly, in my day, we didn't have so many labels. We just called them 'hikers.'"

Many hikers got fired up on this topic. But what it boiled down to, when traveling at least 2,000 miles between Maine and Georgia, was this cliché: "Hike your own hike."

From day one, I decided not to hike somebody else's hike. I would go my own pace, start and end each day when and where I wanted, eat and cook how and what I wished, wear and use whatever gear I desired, and give everyone else the freedom to do the same. I was a quiet Purist and accepted that there was no *one right way* to hike the AT, despite fanatics' insistence otherwise.

The famous Trail Days festival in Damascus, Virginia was less than a week away, and I had well over a hundred miles to cover.

"It's time to hustle, if we're gonna make it on time," I said to some fellow hikers.

"Are you kidding? I'm hitchin' a ride in. That's what you ought to do, too, Small World, if you wanna get there for the kickoff."

"And skip the next hundred miles? No way!" I said.

"No. Just hitch back here after Trail Days, and then continue on through."

My gut told me that coming back south on the Trail from Damascus would be a psychological setback, so I pressed on full force. But the miles were too many. And at my pace I still needed two or three days to reach Damascus... but the festival would begin tomorrow.

Crunch time. What am I to do?

That morning at camp, I overheard some guys planning for the *Damascathon:* a forty-mile stomp from Lake Watauga to Damascus, Virginia. Knowing it was the only way to get there without hitchhiking, my purist ideals were pop-quizzed.

"Is it worthwhile to slack-pack this stretch and reach my goal, or to lose focus and inspiration by coming back south after the festival?" I asked myself.

Do you want to head forward, or tail behind? The coin is flipped, I thought.

"Heads," I called, "for experience points, and to test my trail legs in a new way."

Then heads it shall be.

Together, Funky, The Professor, Butter, Bellows, Smelvin and I laid out the logistics: What would it take to complete such a task? Was it *possible* to trample over forty miles of mountains in one day? Were we conditioned enough? What fuel would we need? Who would take our packs and meet us in Damascus, and at what time? Would we need lights for night hiking?

Smelvin carried a cell phone in his pack, so he called a well-known Trail Angel from Erwin, Tennessee named Miss Janet, who agreed to meet us at Lake Watauga that evening. After a grocery run, all the guys piled into a hotel room for rest, while Miss Janet slept in her van and awaited our 4:30 a.m. wake-up call. Sleep was a far-off dream, as giddiness and anxiety jumped loop-de-loop through my mind.

When the alarm blared, I was convinced I had slept a solid two minutes the entire night. *Thank God for a bumpy van-ride to shake us awake.* Dropping us off at the trailhead next to Lake Watauga, Miss Janet then zipped off to Damascus, promising to set up our tents before the crowds rolled in. The full moon witnessed our first steps around the lake with headlamps and light fanny-packs in place. Mine was a makeshift one, since my backpack's lid did not have the feature of converting into a fanny-pack. With extra shoelaces, I strapped my tent stuff-sack onto my back, using socks to cushion my shoulders. Inside it were a couple Powerbars, dried fruit, peanut butter-spread tortillas, gummy bears, and my Nalgene water container. Full of ambition and high hopes, we set out as a team, amazed at how quickly and easily we traipsed up and down the heights as slack-packers, or "freedom hikers."

Single file we chugged along, but my position in the middle of the train soon became the caboose. Before long, I was alone—left behind in their dust.

"Do it your own way," I reminded myself. "You can catch them when they stop for lunch."

The shelter notebooks gave clues to their progress: *May 18, 2000 - 10:30 a.m. Damascus, here we come! Team Giardia: Funky, The Professor, Butter, Bellows and Smelvin....* But, where was *Small World?* I felt left out, dumped like a carton of bad milk. Discouragement seeped into my legs and doubt soaked my confidence that I could cross the finish line today.

"What I had gotten myself into?" I said to myself... of course—there was *no one else* around to say it to. "I should have listened to my gut."

A breeze slid through the trees.

What did your gut say? said Tree with its always-soothing tone, even when it comes out of nowhere. But I wasn't in the mood to play fetch for answers.

"Oh, Tree..." I whined, "This entire forty mile tromp was a bad idea."

Tree threw the stick again, *Why is that? Specifically? What did your gut actually say?*

I plopped down, picked up Tree's stick and chewed on it like a gopher would until my thoughts rained down on me, flooding my mind with dread and regret. "I should have listened!" I barked. "I just knew the next forty miles may be painful; might be hot; may be rainy; might reach total exhaustion. All during which I may get sleepy; I might get hungry; I may get thirsty; I might get lost... and it's even possible that I may be forced to hitchhike into town. Alone."

Mays and mights, said Tree. *You'll drown if that's all you focus on. By twos your feet came on board this crazy idea, and by twos you'll walk on water if you just keep moving. Don't get cold feet.*

I looked at Tree, stood up, stabbed my hiking poles into the dirt, grit my teeth, and grunted. "This is my hike," I said, "and I'm gonna hike it." And I tackled the Trail two by two: boots and hiking poles marching in rhythm. "Thank you, Tree!" I called.

Two by two, my steps entered "the Zone;" and it reigned for forty "mays" and forty "mights." Its ebb and flow blocked out many storms of pain. Sometimes I looked up, unaware of how far I'd just come. Did I see any of the views? Did I smell any of the flowers? Miles faded away as I plugged along. After one-third complete, I knew I'd make it. I felt fantastic! My lungs, legs, and heart pumped and pulled together like a locomotive engine

"Push it, push it! Go! Go!" I cried.

You couldn't have done this a month or two ago, I thought.

"Look out Damascus, here I come!"

Halfway through, I took an hour-long pit-stop to refuel, rest, and center my focus again. Twenty miles to go. But after the break, my legs puttered and stuttered. A few miles later, feeling drunk with sleepiness, I swerved from side to side on the Trail. Slumped on a log, I cradled my head in my knees. I negotiated with myself for resources beyond what I thought I had. Then somewhere under the hood, the urge to continue cranked up.

Stand. Focus. Breathe. Go!

And I was off…

Many things kept my feet on the Trail (besides the Zone) and away from the growing agony: a cooler full of cookies and soda pop, for example, placed by a Trail Angel. Then I nearly stepped on a rattlesnake stretched across the Trail. There were box turtles, toads, turkey buzzards, and less than ten miles to go.

It was dark, rocky, and eerily quiet. The moon squeezed through the tight-knit trees as I stumbled forward. My headlamp was dimming. *What's that ahead on the Trail?* I tripped on a tree root. *It looks like a signpost.* It was, marking the Tennessee-Virginia state line! I felt exhilarated. I'd followed the border between North Carolina and Tennessee for weeks. Now Damascus, Virginia partied only 3.8 miles away. I was determined to clock in before midnight.

Less than one hour later, I marched into town feeling triumphant, even if on the verge of collapse. Forty-two miles from Lake Watauga, my wristwatch read 11:58 p.m.

I did it.

My boat had landed after a hard Forty Mays and Forty Mights. Trail Days marked a milestone in the AT. And I was there—not to look back, but to look forward: to a couple days of rest… and then to move on from Damascus.

Trail Tidbit #23
Trail Days' Trail Daze

The freshly polished *Damascathon* had buffed me out. All I wanted was a thirty-second *Yeehaw! You did it,* and my tent. Miss Janet had promised to pitch my tent. To find Miss Janet was to find my tent. And everyone knew Miss Janet.

"Where would I find Miss Janet?" I asked a perfect stranger.

"Ah! Miss Janet," he said. "Follow me."

Downtown Tent City hummed like a bee's nest. The city's nightlife pulsated with drummers and dancers around a bonfire. Booze flowed like honey. Smoke bumbled from lips everywhere. Swarms of people had moved to Tent City for the Trail Days weekend: past, present, and future thru-hikers, section-hikers, and day-hikers. Heck, hobos within a hundred miles caught the buzz and blew in, whether hiker or not. Paint a trail blaze on your shirt, and you were in. It was a hive of life-loving, freedom-feeling party animals. Had Trail Days needed a trailname, it would have been Woodstock.

Miss Janet sat surrounded by a dozen hikers, all with a cool drink in hand. I licked my lips and crashed onto the grassy knoll next to them. I heard the first shot: an ice-cold beer can opening beside me.

"Here, you look tired," said my former teammate, Bellows, handing me the beer. I was so bushed-whacked that the beer tasted better than honey. I guzzled it down.

"Thanks, man. I needed that," I said as shot number two cracked.

"Have another." said Funky. "We thought you'd be forced to hitch in."

Bellows added, "I'm impressed. I couldn't have done it without these guys pushing me forward. Congratulations!"

Another beer bulleted towards me, magically fired by someone near the beer depository. I poured it down my throat and hobbled to my tent. Zipping up my tent did not shut out the chalky sweet smell of marijuana and the pre-party racket, but my head hit the floor of my tent sleeping.

Morning arrived at my door with a bouquet of dead flowers. I awoke with a moan, dazed and dehydrated from yesterday's death-march. It didn't help that I had drunk three beers before bed. Blistered, swollen-stiff feet oozed agony. Torture. Every step. First to the port-o-potties. Not the best place to be with a tingling head and a woozy stomach, but when you gotta go... cottage cheese felt like it was hitchhiking up my throat... you gotta go.

Breakfast at Dot's Inn, with Hokey Pokey and B&B (Beth and Bryant), was certain of only one thing: heavy metal music.

Oh, my head... If only the service rocked as much as the jukebox did...

My eardrums kept the beat.

"That guy just picked up his own food from the window," said Beth. "What's with the service here?"

"At least the waitress dances well. Look at her!" I exclaimed.

"I hope she waltzes over here soon," said Hokey Pokey. "I'm hungry."

"I'll get the coffee pot," Bryant said.

"Oh, please do," I said, nursing my secret hangover with a glass of water.

We made Trail-talk while we ate. Beth hoped to be the first woman to complete the entire International Appalachian Trail: the AT plus the extension to Cap Gaspe, Quebec.

"Maybe I'll hike to Key West from Springer Mountain, too. That would be the whole Eastern Continental Divide!" she said.

Ambitious girl, I thought.

"I'll pick up the tab," Hokey Pokey said, "the parade's about to begin."

With rock music ringing in our ears, we left Dot's to find where the Hiker Parade was to begin.

"You guys go on," I said, ripping off my sandals. "I can't go any farther. I'll join the parade when it passes."

The sides of the street were packed with hundreds of townsfolk, curious passers-by, hiker-wannabes, and those too hung over to care. Keeping tradition, police cars lead the parade. Then came clowns. Local Boy Scout troops. A fire truck, blaring its siren. Etc. But what followed was what the masses had come to see. Everyone's neck stretched for a better look. The crowd hushed. A silent mob approached.

Time froze. The ice broke when kilted men lead the throng with bagpipes on cue. Their instruments yodeled a grandiose proclamation, as if heralding the Princess Bride: *Hail to the hikers,* the pipes sang. A thousand hikers strong. The audience roared. My eyes welled, my mouth gaped open. The cheering was for the hikers—for me. I felt proud and honored. I felt a part of something exclusive, unique. I felt pain free in my feet, as the river of hikers swept me away. This was my parade, too.

Like grenades, water balloons catapulted into the air towards bystanders, clowns and other hikers. Squirt guns triggered off in every direction. Nobody but everybody was fair game. A dry guy was a bulls-eye. Anyone who wasn't directly targeted was still riddled with liquid shrapnel ricocheting everywhere around him.

Big wigs, Tarzan rags, gaudy make-up, mud masks, and skirts made of Ramen Noodle pouches decorated the party. Wild. It was Mardi Gras's stepsister, Freakshow. Trail Days 2000 had officially begun.

Gear manufacturers, designers, and vendors of backpacking equipment came to educate and repair broken or worn-out gear (and possibly make a few sales). PUR swapped my water filter for a brand new updated model. The Leki gang gave me new carbide tips for my hiking poles. Mountain Science Research (MSR) cleaned my stove's fuel line. Dozens of booths corralled reps from every conceivable trail-related company: the Appalachian Trail Conference (now known as the Appalachian Trail Conservancy), Backpacker Magazine, Band-Aid. There were chiropractors, artisans, photographers, authors, custom boot cobblers, jewelers, hat and t-shirt stands, and of course food kiosks littered about. The performance stage held shows, talent contests, and lectures. Then came nightfall, when the real partying began.

Up flared the bonfire, and out came the drummers, beating their rhythms into feet and hands. Miss Janet concocted a seven-gallon jug of Long Island Iced Tea. Five thousand beer bottles passed around like loaves and fish among a hungry crowd. Most sojourners whooped it up till they dropped. *Nah!* Not for me, though. Unstick me from the honeycomb and fling me to the side of the busy hive with an occasional margarita and a quiet chitchat. I had been stung once already; that was enough.

Above: Laurel Fork Falls.

Below: At Watauga Lake, Smelvin, Bellows, Funky, Butter, T-Max (1999 thru-hiker), and The Professor and I made plans for The Damascathon.

Trail Tidbit #24
Making Scents

Beauty is in the nose of the beholder. Look up; rhododendrons. Look to the left; mountain laurels. Now to the right; fire azaleas. And down; trilliums. Breathe in. You're on the Appalachian Trail. Do you hear the robin? The scurrying squirrels? Feel the cool breeze on your sweaty skin? Taste the dewdrops dripping from the leaves? Take another breath—through the nose this time. The sense of smell is highly underrated.

A deep whiff of sweet balsam firs hoisted my sagging lungs. Delicious perfumes percolated through the mountainside. I curbed my pace, so I could breathe through my nose. It brought me to new heights after leaving towns, where car exhaust stuck to the walls of my lungs like tar. Trail Days added more toxic smells—weed, beer, hot dogs, and body odor.

A rabble of hikers huddled around Miss Janet, telling stories and jokes.

"There he is!" they hollered like the Paparazzi scouting a celebrity in public. "Small World!"

"Uh, hi…" I smiled.

"You know you're famous now in Erwin!" Miss Janet said.

"Famous? Why?"

"I was carting a bunch of hikers into town when y'all were in Erwin," she continued. "You were going the opposite direction, and with a van-load of hikers, I couldn't pick you up."

Otto jumped in and said, "But you were standing at a big rose bush, sniffing the flowers, with your thumb stuck out in the air for a ride."

"You took time to stop and smell the roses," said Miss Janet. "The entire van cheered and applauded! You didn't hear us?"

"No," I laughed. "What was the big deal?"

"It was the perfect picture of a thru-hiker's priorities! You made our day."

My fame was short-lived, but the countless aromas of the Trail would live in notoriety to the end. It's easy to talk about the sights and sounds, but the sense of smell is often overlooked.

Peas and Carrots

rail Days was also a class reunion—a reunion for the current year of hikers, as well as those from the classes of 1999, 1998, 1997, and so on. We all hoped to catch up with long-lost hiking buddies. I couldn't wait to see Crying Wolf and Lady Kat again. Crying Wolf had pulled ahead of me in the Smokies, and I'd not seen him since. Lady Kat was just a day or two behind me. We had been like three peas in a pod. But Crying Wolf wasn't anywhere to be found, nor heard from again. Thank God Lady Kat made it to Trail Days—I wouldn't see her again on the AT, either. We were split peas.

Journal Entry
5/20/00 - Zero Day #2 in Damascus, VA - Trail Days

Most of my friends are here, except for Crying Wolf. Lady Kat finally showed up, and with aching hips. She's not staying in Tent City, but we met for breakfast and watched the Pacific Crest Trail presentation by Annie and The Salesman. I also filled out my Census 2000 form today, entering "Appalachian Trail" into the address slot.

I'm thrilled to be in Damascus, 450 miles past Springer Mountain,

GA. I remember the stress before setting foot on Georgian soil. I'm thankful for Wingfoot's online AT preparation forum, where I met Sandi. Over the telephone, she had encouraged me not to worry about my weight, conditioning, or finances.

"Go with what you have, how you are," she said. "The rest will come in due course. When I started the Trail, I was 55 pounds heavier, carried a 65-pound pack, and had less than $400. Sure, I didn't make it the whole way, but it was exactly what I needed at that time of my life. When you get to my neck of the woods in Virginia, gimme a shout. We've got a warm shower, a bed, and lots of food! You'll need 'em."

After another 250 miles, I'll look her up. Meanwhile, I've got a party to attend to. Tomorrow's the last day everyone here will be together.

The next day, I was relaxing at a Trail Days exhibit featuring iced tea, lawn chairs, and a cheery stranger, with whom to share some pretzels and small talk. A tarp hung overhead to make shade. A college student joined our cluster to ask questions for her Master's thesis in anthropology. She found us hikers to be an anthropological wonder. Our culture. Our habitat. Our ethics. Our manners. Our philosophies.

"I mean, why on Earth would so many people choose to live like this?" she asked.

"Well, I suppose that some of us cannot really answer that until after we've finished," I said.

"Would you mind if I got your name and e-mail address?" she concluded.

"Small Wor—," I started, "I mean Aaron Welch." I was getting used to my trailname.

That cheery stranger, with whom I shared pretzels and small talk, raised a brow and said, "Why does that name ring a bell? I think I knew someone with that name."

There are several Aarons out there with my last name—no biggie, I thought, and gave the anthropologist my e-mail address.

Something seemed to alight on my new friend's shoulders, for they dropped two inches.

"Now I know," she said, dropping her pretzel, "I'm Sandi!"

My jaw landed in my lap. After the shock fizzled away, I bear-hugged her.

"It is a 'Small World,' after all!" she said.

She handed me her address and telephone number. "You may

spend as much time as you need with me and the kids. And bring a friend or two!"

"I'll be there! You can count on it," I said.

Journal Entry

5/21/00 - Zero Day #3 in Damascus, VA - Trail Days

Tomorrow, Damascus will be clearing out. I hope they were glad to have us... we made a mess (as well as a lot of revenue, I'm sure). Now I'll be in Virginia for a while: 540 miles until the next State line. That's one quarter of the total Trail mileage.

Wingfoot's words are ringing in my ears: "When you reach Virginia, you've paid your dues physically. Next comes the mental and emotional challenge!"

Everyone's got the jitters. "Look out for the Virginia Blues!" they say. "The Middle Miles are legendary for breaking the hardest hikers."

All I can do is put one foot in front of the other. Phase One is behind me, and I don't have to hitch back South to finish uncovered miles. Thank God. I shall jump back in feet first from here.

Sandi's invitation hangs like a carrot in front of me. If I should come down with the Blues, I'll just remember the carrot. Always remember the carrot. Think carrot. Think carrot.

A reunion would indeed occur, and the Blues would turn orange (think carrot). Sandi was one of the greatest sources of edification and a picture of hope. She was the Archangel of Trail Angels. She taught me always to have something to look forward to. Around every bend was a fresh experience.

"Recall what you know is coming," she had said. "Like MacAffee's Knob, the next blueberry patch, or Shenandoah National Park, the next waterfall, or State Line. Make them your next goals. They're all closer than Katahdin."

Don't think Maine. Think carrots.

Top Left: The Traildays Festival hiker parade had begun.

Top Right: Miss Janet made a batch of Long Island iced tea for her friends in Tent City. I'm glad she called me a friend!

Bottom: Yak got beat by a section-hiker! I invited him to Miss Janet's tent, so we could comfort him with some freshly made "tea."

Indoctrinating Tools

Think carrots? Virginia was a virtual carrot patch. Anyone stuck in the Virginia Blues must not have seen them. Carrots, carrots everywhere! Besides waltzing through dreamy tunnels of blooming foliage and marveling over vistas, there were so many ideas to ponder. When in doubt, ask a tree.

"Tree?" I said.

Good morning, Small World, it replied.

I asked, "How do you feel about religion?"

Tree seemed to smile from limb to limb and said, *Ah. Still concerned about heresy, I see. Let me ask you this: Why do you have religions?*

"In general, religions give people's lives purpose and meaning," I answered. "But in the Rat Race, it just hasn't worked well for me. I kept trying and trying, but was never satisfied."

Are you saying that religion never gave you purpose and meaning? asked Tree.

"That's exactly what I'm saying," I said.

Tree replied, *Religion was never meant to create purpose and meaning. Purpose and meaning have always been there. Rather, religion is a tool to point out the purpose and meaning in life.*

"What's the difference?" I asked.

Religion is a means to an end, not the end itself.

"I still don't get it."

Look at your water bottle, Tree said. *Is religion more like the water inside, or the bottle itself?*

I shook my water jar. "Yikes. I don't know." I felt dumber than a log.

According to your reason why you have religions, your answer would be that religion is the water.

"I see. But you're telling me that religion is the bottle, the means to an end."

You got it. It's a tool, said Tree. *Religion also tries to answer the mysteries of the universe.*

"For example?" I asked.

There was a time—not so long ago—that people believed you were demon possessed if you were sick. Then came knowledge seekers who said, "Ah! Germs! Viruses! It's not a demon; it's the flu bug." Or, "Your son isn't possessed, he's got epilepsy."

"Wow! Maybe the realm of the supernatural is simply the Natural finally explained," I said. "And God is the biggest supernatural mystery of all. Is it possible that we will one day uncover God's explanation?"

Tree laughed. *Perhaps, unless God is the thing behind the next answered mystery behind the next answered mystery behind the next answered mystery.... Or, perhaps God is the answers themselves, and we're missing God because the answers don't fit into our paradigm puzzle or cultural equation. Maybe God is the Question, and everyone with all the "answers" therefore completely misses God. All over the world, religion seems to be a tool to hammer out conclusions and answers to mysteries.*

"That doesn't mean I'm rushing back to church," I said.

That's fine, said Tree. *If the hammer is broken, don't fix things with it. Now what tool will you use?*

I wheeled around and patted the Trail behind me. "My present tool is the Appalachian Trail. Yet, I can't put my finger on what the purpose of life is. Here I feel alive and want to live each day. I want the serendipity that exploration brings. I want to touch, taste, see, hear, smell, think, and feel new and mysterious things."

Tree leaned in and whispered, *Small World, you've just put your finger on the purpose of life.*

"I did? What is it?" I asked.

With mighty hands stretched out, and chest lifted high, Tree bellowed, *The purpose of life is to live!*

Trail Tidbit #27
Fermented Ethics

The Trail is like your local tavern. *What'll you have, mister? Sky's the limit.* Sometimes you get a drink straight up. *Oh, it burns.* Sometimes you get it on the rocks, or with a twist. *Ow, my ankle!* Sometimes you get it mixed with sweet-and-sour. *Rain, shine, rain, shine.* Sometimes you get a stiff drink. *Man, this guy is a piece of work!* And some drinks just don't mix.

Thru-hikers tended to think of themselves as the Dom Pérignon of the Trail. Section-hikers, as arrogant as it might sound, were often treated like house wines. Don't get me wrong—many were very pleasant, but we all seemed to have different standards. We didn't always sit on the same table together.

I'm no connoisseur, so I gave most house wines a chance. Pilgrim was a section-hiker from Florida. He was a professor of philosophy. Good wine! We were having an evening chat alone at Old Orchard shelter when an older fellow named Jake dropped in.

"My, my," he muttered in his James Earl Jones voice, "I'm tuckered out."

We welcomed him to the rickety shelter, trying to ignore the awful sound echoing within his barrel chest as a result of post-nasal crash.

Snort! H-k-h-k-k!

I looked at Pilgrim to see if he'd heard what I'd just heard. He looked away, shirking a grin. He'd heard. It sounded as if Jake gargled a thick hollandaise sauce after every third breath.

Pilgrim and I preferred the outside edges of shelters next to the walls, so a couple meters between us was open for him.

"I'd like to lay crosswise up at the back," he said, with his hand waving toward the rear wall of the shelter. *Snort!*

"Well, that would either put your feet in one of our faces, or our feet in yours," we tried to explain, politely telling him just to sleep like a normal person, lengthwise into the shelter. He didn't like the idea too much.

"That's okay," he said. "I've hiked all over this nation and find that I prefer sleeping out under the stars, really."

"Stars? It's going to rain," I said, as thunder rolled above.

H-k-h-k-k! replied Jake. He grabbed his gear and napped down in the small meadow out front. No tent, no tarp, just a poncho. Within minutes, streaks of rain sent Jake scurrying back to the shelter with his sleeping bag suspended over his head.

Tried to tell ya, I thought.

The self-proclaimed seasoned hiker didn't act as if he had any trail-sense whatsoever. I don't know what he was thinking; the lights in the sky were not stars, they were lightning bolts. And why did he leave his backpack and food out in the meadow to get drenched? To launder his clothes and soak his beans? Somehow I thought not. Jake was a stiff drink.

"Would one of you boys mind fetching my gear out there?" Jake asked. Pilgrim and I gazed at each other, blinking in disbelief.

Has he never hiked in rain before? I thought. *Seasoned hiker, my ass!*

A passerby had overheard Jake's prayer and offered to save him. Thank God. But Jake was praying the Rosary and had many beads to go. He petitioned for favors until we'd pretended we'd fallen asleep.

"Could you please open this? *Snort!* Would you get my hot water for me? *Snort!* Hand me my water, son. *Snort!* Here, please hold my flashlight while I… oh—*snort*—I got it," he said, seeing that we were "sleeping."

For the next half hour Jake fumbled with his pack, clattered his cookware, and beat his boots. This was no mere house wine, this was grape juice. *H-k-h-k-k! H-k-h-k-k!* Make that a mere grape. It took all my strength not to trample the grapes of wrath, while his flashlight beam flickered in my eyes again and again. I dropped hints by dramatically covering my eyes and puffing exasperated sighs. He never got the point.

What if he snores? I thought.

Jake snored. One long, loud, everlasting, ear-crunching, continuous *H-k-h-k-k!*

Jake came to life in the morning and immediately began to fiddle and snort. By the time Pilgrim and I rose from the dead, we'd been ordered a dozen commands.

"Please put my poncho over on that boulder to dry. Would you crush my soup can? Check to see if my tea pot blew away, I don't see it."

Ready to pop a cork, Pilgrim and I scrammed without breakfast, but not without a glimmer of satisfaction. I had something to confess to Pilgrim.

"Did you notice Jake hanging his food-bag on that nail in the shelter last night?" I asked.

"Yes, but I wasn't going to say anything," he admitted.

"Me neither. He's gotta learn somehow."

You see, most shelters are strung with food-hangers to keep food-bags away from little food-nabbers below. But since mice will also crawl down the line from above, the string is threaded through the center of an aluminum can. When the mouse reaches the can, not only can he not proceed down the line, but he's also likely to slip off. Apparently, Jake was ignorant of this bit of technology when he draped his food sack over a nail on the wall.

Pilgrim and I pled guilty of knowing he'd have trouble by morning. All night long, alongside Jake's snoring, we had heard mice chewing holes in *someone's* bag. Not mine. Not Pilgrim's. We never said a word. A bad wine isn't worth saving. Smirking, we had left the grape out to dry like a raisin. And although I like raisins, they weren't much good without nuts or cereal. And we weren't about to let him into our oatmeal.

Trail Tidbit #28
Apple-achian Amigo

Since one day's space on the Trail was potentially an eternity between hikers, I often met new northbound faces throughout the entire route. Sometimes familiar faces would resurface after months of separation.

Well over six hundred miles past Springer Mountain, just outside Pearisburg, Virginia, lay Rice Field shelter. Sitting in a large cow meadow atop the mountain, I relaxed with my journal while waiting for dusk.

Journal Entry
6/8/00—From Pearisburg, VA to Rice Field Shelter (6.8 miles)

I am now sitting on a big rock, overlooking a vast West Virginian valley. The Trail straddles the State line here. Wild strawberries speckle the ground around me, and cows moo not far away. I'm waiting on this perfect eve for the sunset... it should be great.

Just a few moments ago, as I was writing this, who should walk up but Bear! He was slack-packing southward.

"Small World?" I heard him call from behind me, "It's The Bear." Oi! It was the ultra-lightly packed incorrigible Bear. He'd slimmed down and wore his cap, sunglasses and spandex (God save us), so I hardly recognized him.

"What are you doing in these parts?" I asked, thinking he was weeks ahead.

"This is my home," he said. "I had to get off the Trail in Damascus, because my mother was critically ill." He continued to tell me how he held his mother's hand as she died. "Getting back on the Trail has been hard."

I told him I was sorry to hear this, and he waved good-bye. I returned to my journal. Moments later, someone else called from behind me: "Hey there, Small World!"

It was a chap who'd woven in and out of my path only recently, a newer face. I'd camped near him once and made small talk with him at the Woodshole Hostel near Pearisburg, but I didn't know his name. I was surprised he knew mine. He was one of many who was "hiking his own hike..." so, why should I have bothered him?

"Hey! Come on over," I said, as if to an old friend, waving him over to my rock. "I'm sorry, I don't remember your name."

"Apple," he said, "I'm Apple. Gonna watch the sunset?"

"Yeah, why don't you hang out and enjoy it yourself?"

"Sounds great, but I haven't done my minimum for the day. I should keep going."

"Me neither!" I shrugged. "Who cares? The sunsets are supposed to be spectacular from up here."

I coaxed Apple into staying. He's cooking his supper at this very moment, while I write this all down. I wonder how he got his trailname...

"How'd you get your trailname, Apple?" I asked.

"Well, I managed Red Jacket Apple Orchard for two years until I started the Trail. Did you know Rascal and Sunny? We hiked together my first week on the Trail. One day I pulled out an apple to get me up and over Blood Mountain. Sunny couldn't believe I had carried an apple for 60 miles before eating it. I told her all about apples and which ones are the best. Rascal thought I knew too much about them and began calling me 'Appleman.' Sunny dropped the 'man,' and there, then, and from that moment on, I was known on the AT as 'Apple.'"

Apple knows about more than just apples; the things he knows about the cows around us tonight is astonishing. Apple grew up in Upstate New York on a farm and studied Agriculture Economics, Small Business Management, and Marketing at Cornell University. Quite impressive.

He seems like a good guy. I hope to see more of him on the Trail.

It came as a surprise to me how much I would indeed see him on the Trail: we would go through highs and lows together, weathering storms, fording rivers, and eating countless bags of Ramen noodles together.

Twenty-four-sevens together would teach how to annoy, edify, heckle, and motivate each other. Apple and I would hold serious debates and even learn to cut loose (if you catch my drift) when manners no longer mattered. We would joke about everything from yellow-blazers to idiosyncrasies, which we each owned (he more than I, of course). For example, Apple always whistled exclamations.

"Would you look at that sunset!" I'd say.

Apple would whistle, as if to say "Wow!"

Or, "I paid over forty dollars for my titanium pot."

Apple would flute a "No way!"

Although he was long-winded, Apple also seemed to articulate better with his hands than with his mouth. Waving hands and pointing fingers escorted his phrasing like an air-traffic controller. I suggested he become a choir conductor, but the poor guy carried a tune like a saddle carried a horse.

When I discovered his strong points and passions, however, he was as fluent as a lawyer and eloquent as a poet. He knew a lot about public relations, business procedures, management, and marketing. Highly gifted, Apple could cater pork chops at a Bar Mitzvah. Consulting was his specialty. It spilled over into his personal life, too. Countless times I bounced ideas off him or asked for his advice. He had a knack for seeing the invisible and envisioning ways to accomplish the impossible.

I liked his company on my way north. This was mutual from the start. Apple was to become a companion whose friendship and influence I would greatly value. Off trail, common grounds were dissimilar landscapes, but our mutual goal on the Trail would see us through all topographies.

Trail Tidbit #29
Squatter's Refuge

Believe it or not, books are written to address the issue of answering Nature's Call in the Outdoors. Authors have made it their duty to appease peoples' potty phobias. Potty training took practice, and in time it was as simple as "#1, 2, 3." I became pretty regular with the "squatty potty" method. It was handier than the porcelain manner, although most Trail shelters had outhouses, ("privies" in AT lingo). They were not as fragrance-free and readily available as the self-made ones but offered privacy and humor when at camp.

Creativity built privies with drawbridge doors, composting or ventilation systems, psychedelic paint jobs, mock flush handles, mirrors, even reading material. Some privies sat over picturesque vistas, while others offered claustrophobic settings, triggering the gag reflex. There were always memorable favorites and unforgettable horrors.

Piazza Rock Lean-to, built by L.L. Bean, named their privy "Your Move Privy," which was not only built for two, but also had a game board between pots. Hikers often dubbed a privy to match its virtues (and vices). There was the Leaning Tower of Pee-sa at Trapper John Shelter. I don't know how anyone sat in that one. Sassafras Gap shelter owned the Dilapidated Dung Domicile. I named Bailey Gap shelter's privy the "Indy 500," because the swarming flies buzzed like a day at the races upon "take off."

Getting used to quick cat-holes and plenty of trees, the bladder adapts to free reign. There's no waiting, no lines, no worries in the woods. When you gotta go, you gotta go, so you just... go. Problem was, while in towns, after months of such blissful bowel behavior, I could hardly contain myself. "Ignore it, and it will go away" no longer worked. My plumbing only heard, "On your mark. Get set. Go!" And now! Oh, the pain, the dread, the fear of failure and humiliation. I was a refugee, running for my life. *Where do I go now?* The books never put the lid down on that question. I had to find my own squatter's refuge, my own pot to piss in. I learned (not the hard way, thank goodness) always to scope out an escape plan.

Everything flushed out in the end, although I was always glad to be back in the woods, where I was as free as the birds, squirrels, and bears to do in the woods what bears do in the woods to answer every affirmative question.

Trail Tidbit #30
Watered Down

A creek licked the toes of my boots. I sucked water through the bite-valve of my Platypus hydration-system strapped to my backpack with a tube that snaked around to my mouth. It was flowing easily, so I figured it had enough water to last me until the next spring or creek. There was always water nearby when I ran out of it. Always. Besides, I didn't feel like dumping the bothersome beast on my back to filter-pump water now. So, I hopped over the creek and carried onward.

The sun pounded nails into my skin. My Platypus was dry. So was the Trail.

Since when did water have an expiration date on the AT? I thought. *Water.*

Every last ounce of sweat baked onto my skin. I crawled up the mountain.

Water...

My head bloated, as if being filled with a tire pump. For miles I sucked the dusty air for traces of moisture.

Waa-ter.

Wa—

Chipper gurgles. Gushing burbles.

"Water!" I wheezed, crashing over rocks and fallen branches toward the sound of crisp, cold, precious, living water. I sat at a spring that welled right over the Trail and began pumping my PUR water filter. Pump, pump, pumping—*If this were a river, I'd jump in!*—nothing but air swish, swish, swished.

"Piece of shit!" I screeched. *What now?* I didn't dare drink straight from the spring. It might have been contaminated with giardia: the most dreaded dyspeptic virus of all. *I should have gotten water when I had the chance.* Now I was painfully thirsty. Little did I know that the pump simply needed to be primed. Why I hadn't needed to prime it before was beyond me.

Despite this one episode, PUR seemed to make the best water filter on the Trail. Whenever my filter cartridge became dirty and clogged, PUR replaced it for free. To save weight, some hikers carried iodine tablets. Apple used a small dropper-bottle of Clorox bleach. Light and efficient. Others drank unfiltered spring water and risked ingesting a giardia virus, which would force them off the Trail with cramps, diarrhea and nausea.

Spring water was sweet and delicious. The only thing that competed for water's attention was Gatorade. According to Gatorade marketers, water doesn't replace sweat in the body. Sweat is not only water, but also is potassium and sodium: electrolytes. Why drink water if you can drink sweat?

Hail Gatorade! I gulped gallons of it.

Fresh from gas-station coolers when in town or mixed from my own powdered supply, it became a daily luxury well worth its weight. To tell the truth, however, nothing could replace the elegant essence and pristine pleasure of honest, all-natural water. My body pleaded for its lubricating, cleansing purity and inherent energy. And why not? The body is about 80% water—not salt and potassium. I'd heard it said that the human body is an invention of water, so that the water could get up and walk around. Bathing in it now and then was good, too.

Apple and I lasted for days with sweat-caked skin. Maybe we just got used to it or were dabbling nostalgically with our bygone boyhood. Salty residue scraped our brows like sandpaper. If "cleanliness is next to godliness," then we were heathens to the core. Nonetheless, an occasional shower from Heaven was blissful, no matter how much I loathed hiking in the rain.

Apple and I marched up Apple Orchard Mountain, when for once we cheered the driving rains as it flushed us clean. We passed under The Guillotine (a boulder suspended between two monoliths). Miles later, we stopped at Thunder Ridge shelter to gather drinking water, eat a snack, and dump out our boots. The sun popped out. By the time we geared up to hike again, we were dry. It was late afternoon. There were a couple hours of good hiking daylight left, so we moved onward.

"Man, I'm about to start sweating again. I just had a shower!" I half-jokingly complained.

Apple replied, "Well, if we run, we'll get there before we sweat!"

Hiking the Appalachian Trail was hard work. There was no way around sweating. I sweated buckets-full. Most of my fat was lost through the floodgates of my skin. And I was proud of that. I sweated in my shirt and shorts so much in one day that they wrung out like a sponge. It sopped in my boots, dripped off my ears, nose, beard, and brows and into my eyes, and it matted my hair. But water—cherished water—diluted all my problems, washing my slate clean.

How did I ever take this abundant resource for granted? Water was like a rescue buoy to the drowning. Dipping my toes in a pool, sipping a long fulfilling drink, dripping it on my head, and equipping my containers for the long haul in a dry season, I learned to love water as a best friend. We became inseparable. Water was the spice of Trail life.

Top Left: Grayson Highlands State Park contained Virginia's highest peak, Mt. Rogers: 5,729' and feral horses. Just as I had felt skittish around the long-horned cattle, these horses were skittish of me. I have no spikes sticking out of my head, no flashy rings in my nose (or anywhere else), and I am modest about exposing my... you know. So, I wondered why they were afraid.

Bottom Left: Breakfast at Tillie Woods' Woodshole Hostel consisted of Apple, Wildman, Joe Cool, Scott, Nora, Paisley, eggs, biscuits and gravy, sausage, grits, coffee and me.

Right: Spring had entered the trees and pushed out the leaves. Distant views were now rare.

Trail Tidbit #31
The Apple Core

I dumped a packet of Ramen noodles into my pot. "Apple? Can I ask you a personal question?" I asked.

"Sure." Apple smiled.

"Why did you come to the Trail?"

Apple's shoulders dropped, and he bowed his head. "To pursue a dream," he said.

He looked sad and lost. His body language hinted that there was something deeper. I waited and listened.

"My wife and I are separated," he continued. "Things were getting rough."

I stirred my noodles.

"I don't want a divorce."

"What does she want?" I asked.

"Time. We need time to figure things out. Meanwhile, we're both chasing dreams."

"What's her dream?"

"She went back to school," Apple said.

"And your dream is thru-hiking the AT?"

Apple paused and sighed. "I've always wanted to hike the AT," he said. "But my dream is my wife. I'm pursuing her."

I sipped a spoonful of broth.

"This is my pilgrimage, too." Apple said. "I'm looking for new life. Even a new outlook on things."

"You're in the right place for that," I said.

After an Apple-classic whistle, he said, "I've learned so much already. Out here you learn what you value, what you take for granted, what is *real.*"

I couldn't agree more, but all I managed to say was "Yeah" with another slurp of soup.

"My wife," Apple said. "It's my wife. She is why I came to the Trail."

Trail Tidbit #32
Silence is Golden

t exploded out of nowhere. I never heard it coming. Absolute serenity, amplified under a dome of tranquility, roared in my ears. Even awe played Mum's the Word. My mind was the only noisemaker; I scrutinized the soundlessness. Was it possible for the world to know this quietude? It came as a foreigner to the metropolis between my ears. Was I too populated to let this stranger take residence? My spine tingled like wet skin in a breeze.

What's on your mind? asked Tree, whose voice never broke the silence.

"I'm thinking about silence," I answered.

Tree laughed. *Sounds counterproductive. What are you thinking about the silence?*

"You said the Bible has a lot to say, but suppose it didn't say everything?"

That's quite likely, Tree answered. *Anything that has* everything *to say usually says everything but* anything *at all. In other words, anything that presumes to be the end-all is usually the end of itself.*

I thought it best not to ask him to repeat that or to explain it…. "In my upbringing," I said, "some of my teachers said that if the Bible didn't say it, then it must not be for us to know, because everything we need to know—everything that was *meant* for us to know—is in the Word of God. Can you believe that?"

Hm. Do you really think your curious mind was intended to go to waste? This is a battle that has been fought for hundreds, if not thousands, of years, Tree said. *And the ones armed with this argument always lose, because the rest of the world refuses to remain stagnant.*

"Really?" I said. "How so?"

Do you remember anything about Galileo?

"A little bit. He built a telescope," I said, "and found moons circling Jupiter."

That's right. He built a telescope, because he was curious. What else had been known about Jupiter before the telescope was invented? asked Tree.

I nibbled my bottom lip. "I don't know," I said.

How was Jupiter different from most other lights in the night sky?

I lit up and shouted, "It moved!"

Tree whistled in the breeze and said, *Exactly. That's what the word* planet *means: wandering. Galileo's curiosity discovered facts with his telescope that stirred up bitter emotions among many people.*

"Yes! I get it!" I howled. "Most people believed what they saw in the Eastern sky every morning—that the sun revolved around the earth. Galileo gave overwhelming evidence to confirm Copernicus's theory that planet Earth wasn't the center of the universe after all."

Right on, said Tree. *You can almost hear Galileo's thoughts: "Jupiter moves across the sky, is round and has orbiting moons. We believe our moon orbits Earth, but Jupiter moves across the sky. That's it! We're moving! The sun doesn't move; rather we orbit the sun, rotating on an axis, just as Jupiter does!"*

"It seems so elementary nowadays," I said. "But Galileo had ferocious opponents to his theory, whom treated the Bible like a scientific treatise."

That's right, said Tree. *They believed that truth could* only *be found in those pages.*

"The author of Ecclesiastes said that the *sun* rises and sets and goes around to rise again. The Psalmist wrote that God had put the earth on an immovable foundation."

Psalm 93 and 104, added Tree. *They dealt with the same card you're now struggling with.*

"Which card is that?" I asked.

They believed what they saw in the Bible. It's the "But the Bible says..." card. Yet some of Galileo's opponents understood that the Bible used figurative language. But they still held out their best card: "The Bible didn't say it..." So, they didn't accept Galileo's theories either.

"It was the Bible's *silence* that stuck them," I said. "What about the stuff you've been teaching me? Don't you form the Bible around your beliefs?" I asked.

Do my teachings (or shall we call them ideas?) contradict the Bible, in your opinion? Tree asked.

"They may or may not. My point is that you're teaching me things that the Bible doesn't even address."

Tree said, *And so my ideas are probably not true. Is that your conclusion?*

"No. It just seems that the Bible is silent about them. That's all.

Silence is no surprise, Small World. Much of the world has forgotten how to learn from silence. "If silence is nothingness, then it must have nothing to say," they think. Don't let your mind get stuck. Let it evolve. Why do you think that Galileo's people's minds were stuck?

"I guess they were afraid that curiosity would kill their cats," I said.

Tree snickered, *Very funny. But I know what you mean. People are invested in what they believe. Mentally. Emotionally. Spiritually. New thoughts and ideas from a curious mind may make you question your beliefs too deeply.*

"Their interpretation of the Bible was shaken. Their theology. Their dogma. Galileo let a cat out of the bag, and it chased their dogma around in circles!" I said. "We were God's special creation and everything revolved around *us*."

Not the sun then, said Tree.

"Nope. The Bible made it clear that it was all about us. Now Galileo's innocent curiosity threatened all that. So they branded him a heretic."

Tree shook its leaves and said, *And Galileo ultimately won! Truth always does, wherever it's found. Just because the Bible doesn't spell it out, doesn't mean we're not meant to read between the lines or that truth cannot be found elsewhere, independent of the Bible's support.*

"So, what if scientific proofs actually do contradict the Bible? Most of my teachers also said that if a teaching contradicted the Bible, then the teaching was false."

We've seen how this is dangerous and sometimes silly. It seems that if the Bible were the only source of truth, then people interpretations of it are whacked. But somehow I think that the Bible was not intended to be read like an almanac or science textbook. It's not a thermometer or a telescope or a clock or a scale or a magic crystal ball. So, why humans try to make it be all things to them is a wonder to me. They leave no room for God to reveal anything else about himself... or herself, for that matter, or by any other means. They've got God all caged up and figured out.

I may be going out on a limb here, said Tree, *but it's full of fear.*

"Fear of the Natural," I said. "If the supernatural is explained, then it might be possible, they fear, someday to explain God," I said.

That's the strange thing, said Tree. *If we indeed have curious minds, and we explain those mysteries, and we understand that, which was once "supernatural," then we might know God more. Knowing God would become* natural...

"...And God would *become* as natural as we are, and we wouldn't want that!"

Or vice versa; we might realize the divinity in *us.*

"I get tired of jumping from fear to false humility to pretentiousness to egotism, trying to claim to understand the dogma and doctrines I grew up with. It's all so noisy and dizzying."

And truth is lost. Although all truth is one truth.

"Yes. Truth is truth is truth," I said. "All truths fall under the category Truth, whether scientific or metaphysical."

That's right. Just as all mankind fall under the category of Human Race. And all mankind is seeking truth.

"If all mankind is seeking truth," I said, "then what kind of god would God be, if he withheld truth from those seeking it? What kind of god would God be, if he gave it all to one race and none to another race and expected us to work out the difference? What kind of truth would Truth be, if it manifested itself in one people groups' worldview and culture, and not across the globe?"

I'm stumped, said Tree. *We all have found truth. None of us have all of it. There's more to find. Scientists call them discoveries, and clergymen call them revelations. They shape our minds and hearts. The discovery of Earth's orbit around the sun required you to change your mind about your position in the universe. Some religious folks tried to change this discovery to match their theology, and they lost. When revelations and discoveries are made, it is our duty to change our interpretations of truth, not change the truth to fit our beliefs.*

"If there is a God, then I don't believe the Bible is the only word he spoke."

As the world evolves, no good god would stay mute. If God wants us to know him, then he must satisfy our exploring minds. That's what the word "science" means: knowledge. Remember, too, that the Bible authors weren't asking the same questions you are. Nor did they have a language with which to ask.

"Language? What do you mean?"

Listen. What is the smallest particle you've ever seen?

"I've seen amoebas and other one-celled critters under a microscope."

Do you think the ancient Hebrew authors of Genesis knew what a cell was? Not even Charles Darwin grasped it. He called it a "black box." The smallest particle a Hebrew person could have seen was a speck of dust. "Man was made from the dust of the ground" is not too far fetched from an evolutionary point of view, if a linguistic light is thrown on it.

"In fact," I said, "on the fifth and sixth days of Creation, the original language doesn't say that God created the living creatures of the sea and earth; rather, it says the *waters* and *earth* brought them forth. And there's a difference between *create* and *make*, too; God didn't create man; he *made* him!"

Maybe the Bible isn't as silent as it initially seems, Tree said.

"Then again," I said, "you can make it say whatever you want it to say."

True enough. Perhaps truth is found not in the words of the world's scriptures themselves, but rather in their silence. It's a still small voice. Let that stillness shape you.

My boots danced a hypnotizing tempo up the Trail, where the silent woods spoke volumes. I felt like a garden seed, buried in that dark quiet place, fixing to sprout and blossom. Ah, the silence was golden.

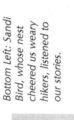

Top Left: Two Brits, Mad Dog and Cupcake, took a break to debate the proper way to make tea.

Bottom Left: Sandi Bird, whose nest cheered us weary hikers, listened to our stories.

Right: Reaching McAfee Knob was finally to snatch a huge carrot that had been dangling in front of me for hundreds of miles. "It looks rather misty; I think a storm is coming." Yes! I saw lightning… below me!

Trail Tidbit #33
Sticks and Stones

Dragon's Tooth was a massive quartzite pillar that jutted out of the ground above the trees. It was just a few miles away from the Catawba Grocery & Gas Station, where I called Sandi. The carrot was thunk.

"Sandi's leaving work to come get us," I said. "She says to give her thirty minutes."

Apple and I scarfed down ice cream sandwiches and Gatorade.

"It's fricking hot out here," Apple said, wiping his forehead with his bandana. "I'm going back into the gas station."

It was a good excuse for another ice cream sandwich.

Two Englishmen, Steve and Mad Dog, shuffled inside, sniffing for treats. They bickered for twenty minutes about the best English sports teams and the proper way to make tea. It was North against South. Lancaster versus London. When Sandi pulled in, she screamed with delight, when we all crammed into her car.

"It'll be a full house tonight!" she said.

"Oh, we wouldn't want to impose," said Steve. "A local bed-n-breakfast should do fine."

Leave manners to the Brits, I thought.

"Baloney," Sandi laughed. "Save your money. Take a zero day, or two, at my place."

On our zero-day, Steve and I walked to K-mart for groceries and to borrow their scales.

"Wow! Forty pounds in 2.5 months!" I cheered.

Steve took a scale off the shelf and tiptoed onto it.

"Aw, I ought to go try on the bras!" he bellowed. "Stupid scale. At least... I must have come down a couple *cup* sizes." He squeezed his chest in both hands, disappointed in his progress towards weight-loss.

We meandered through the store shopping for trailwares, when we passed the lingerie section. Steve grabbed a bra and said, "I ought to call myself '*Cup*cake'."

"That's it! You said it... it's stuck! Your trailname is Cupcake!" I said. We chortled to tears, even after the cashier scowled at us.

Cupcake had me in stitches all the time. It was his horribly dry wit, British antics, and quirky habits. Sometimes it was his gas. Cupcake farted without shame. *Whatever happened to English manners?* Our second slack-pack day began with a bang: Cupcake's every step up the mountain towards Fullhardt Knob shelter quacked.

"My, perhaps I should compose a symphony," he said.

Quack, quack, quack...

"Geez, Cupcake," I replied, "make it the Finished Symphony!"

"No, sir," he said. "This one will leave a mark!"

We both lost it. I buckled to my knees laughing; Cupcake quacked to his.

Cupcake always pulled his shorts up over his thighs, like a speedo, so they wouldn't catch while hiking uphill. His t-shirt hung low, as if he wore a sundress. Two short legs poked straight out under the dress. The stares he got from other hikers were just as comical.

Mad Dog was in the shelter when we got to there. I crashed in its shade and yanked out my water bottle. Cupcake used the privy.

"What's taking Cupcake so long?" I asked after a quart of water.

"I hope that's a rhetorical question," Mad Dog answered.

I chucked a pebble at the privy.

"Ai!" hollered Cupcake.

Then a regular stone.

"What the—? What's going on out there?" he yelled.

I whipped another rock at the privy, which nearly smacked him in the head as he exited.

He slammed the privy door and said, "I've got a riddle for you."

"No," I said. "My stomach hurts from laughing too hard."

"What's brown and sticky?" he asked anyway.

"Oh, brother. You're asking me that, after this morning's Surprise Symphony?"

"A stick, you twit!" he said.

I honestly don't know why it struck me so funny, but I nearly sprang a leak. I ran to the privy.

Cupcake took the pitcher's mound for revenge.

BAM!

I hadn't realized it was possible to jump from a sitting position.

BAM!

BAM!

From inside, each stone made a resounding echo, startling me. I couldn't see the rocks coming. Then the Southerner, Mad Dog, united with his fellow countryman.

B-BAM!

B-BAM!

One of them flung a handful of pebbles at the privy.

BAM-b-b-b-BAM-BAM!

I about died. It's not a good thing to laugh so hard inside a privy, let me tell you... you could asphyxiate.

That was Cupcake's last day on the Trail. I missed him for weeks. His section-hike was too short, as far as I was concerned. News from Sandi reported that he'd gotten Lyme Disease. Cupcake had recognized the symptoms after returning to England, but doctors wouldn't take Cupcake's word for it. I wanted to send him a get-well gift from the Trail. I thought about tying a pretty ribbon around a stick from Virginia, tagged with a note: "What's brown and sticky?"

Trail Tidbit #34
Angelic Behavior

Handwritten Sign

THRU-HIKERS, HELP YOURSELVES!
-YOUR LOCAL TRAIL ANGEL

Bumping into a cooler pregnant with sodas, cookies, sandwiches or fruit was as exciting as spotting my Easter basket as a kid. More times than not, though, I lifted the lids of empty Styrofoam boxes, except for ants and potato bugs, which was like waking up Christmas morning to find a lump of coal in your stocking. Nonetheless, sterile coolers made it more thrilling when one turned up fertile.

Apple and I dropped 3,000 feet toward the Tye River in Virginia. When we landed at the foot of the mountain, I noticed a red and white box sitting under a bush.

"I'll play Gyno," I said to Apple. I bent over the box and opened her up. "She's pregnant!"

The fruit of her womb bore two crescent moons of luscious honeydew melon.

"Twins! One for you, one for me," I said, delivering a slice to Apple.

"Leave the Jim Beam," Apple said. "Alcohol is a diuretic, and we've got another 3,000 footer to climb, across the river."

More energizing than a cooler's goodies was the spark of serendipity; that feeling of luck when finding wonderful things not looked for. It felt as if *someone* was watching over us. Trail Angels.

Sometimes a cooler would find *us*. Several hikers were relaxing in a roadside park.

"Do you hear that?" I asked.

It sounded like giant wings beating the air.

"It's coming closer."

A sports car screeched to a halt beside us. A bass beat shook its tinted windows. The music amplified as the driver's door opened, and a cool chap with sunglasses sprung out. "You guys thru-hikers?"

An Angel. Disguised with shades and hot-wheels. Odd, perhaps, but at least the car was white.

"I got some beers in the trunk!" he hollered.

Every last one of us bolted for the car.

The Angel introduced himself, "T-Max. I thru-hiked last year. Yo, I got a grill, too. Y'all hungry? How 'bout some burgers and dogs?"

Did a thru-hiker ever turn down free food?

Most Trail Angels, who performed these miracles, knew what hikers loved. They delighted themselves in materializing foods and beverages flowing with calories and taste. Some Angels, however, were rookies and didn't realize that the reason hikers liked rich foods was because they *needed* them.

"Hey, Small World!" Apple called, "Look what I found! Fruit and sodas in a bag, hanging on this tree!"

"All right!" I said, speeding towards the jackpot.

"There's a note here from Cool Hand Luke and Fennel. I guess a Trail Angel gave them all this."

"Yeah? Great! What's all in there?" I asked.

"Apples. Oranges. Here," Apple said, handing me a soda and an orange.

"Strawberry-kiwi pop, eh?" I said, ogling the label on the can.

"Yup. It's diet," said Apple.

"Diet? Is there anything else in the bag?"

"Nope, just diet," Apple sighed, pawing through the stash.

"Oh. Well, let's see," I shrugged, rotating the can to read its nutrition facts, as Apple cracked his open. "Hm. Zero calories, zero sodium, zero carbohydrates...."

Apple smacked his lips, "And zero taste, too! I can't drink this stuff."

"Ugh!" I agreed with one sip, pouring mine out. "How's your apple, Apple?"

"Soft. Dry. How's your orange?"

"Crunchy."

"No wonder Cool Hand Luke and Fennel left all this here," Apple laughed.

"I think that Angel just recently received his wings!"

Angels manifested themselves in the South more than in the North. Even hitchhiking in the North was toilsome. But Angels everywhere would give the halos off their heads! An Angel named Tom served an ornate dish of ice-cream, topped with whipped cream and dinosaur sprinkles, and a slice of cantaloupe on a silver platter and doily. Other Angels, traveling Skyline Drive, made communion with cheese and iced tea. They invited me to their home in New Jersey. One saintly lady manifested a twenty-dollar bill, insisting we buy ourselves a proper meal in town. Perhaps the truth was, she was worried about her own son—hiking overseas—and hoped for good karma.

North or South, angels united in purpose for the benefit of us mortals on the Appalachian Trail. Whether with pancakes, cold cuts, or lifts into town, they rarely expected thanks, never accepted gas money, nor ever judged us according to appearance. Trail Angels were ever-encouraging sources of hope and strength; shepherds to a weary soul.

Trail Tidbit #35
Taste of His Own Medicine

A dusty mirage sat on the Virginian meadows. Tall grasses scraped our legs, as we plowed through them. It was hot.

"When's dinner?" I said. "I'm starving."

"You're always hungry," Mad Dog replied.

"My tooth aches!" Apple barked.

"Your tooth always aches, Apple."

"Mine doesn't," said Mad Dog.

We pitched camp near Sinking Creek and dug out our cooking gear. One by one, stars peeped out of the twilight-blue heavens. A cool night was falling. I caught a fresh breath of air and ripped off a bite of jerky. There was nothing like suppertime.

"My tooth is still bothering me," Apple said.

"Don't you have anymore pain-relief crème?" I asked.

"Yeah, I just bought a new tube of it in town."

Apple unzipped his backpack lid, where he kept toiletries, and took out the medicine. After squeezing a dab onto his finger, he shoved it in his mouth and scrubbed his gums where his tooth hurt. Suddenly, he looked up with a cocked expression and read the label on the tube.

Pa-tooh! Pt! Pt! he spat.

"What! What is it?" I asked him.

"I bought the wrong stuff," he said. "This is for cold sores!"

Perhaps I had the best laugh.

"I thought it tasted weird," Apple said.

"At least it isn't hemorrhoidal crème," Mad Dog said.

Mad Dog was first to roll up his tent in the dewdrop morning. Apple washed oatmeal slime from his pot. I skimmed through my Trail Companion book.

"Oh, finally," I said. "Today we get to see the Keffer Oak. It's over 300 years old and at least 18 feet around!"

Apple puckered his lips and fifed a *Holy Cow!*

"See ya up the Trail," I said.

The stoic oak stood like George Washington crossing the Delaware River on the bow of his boat. Magnanimous. Tall. A white blaze scarred its body but not its spirit. Queen of the Forest. She spread her mighty arms over me to shield me—a mere peasant—from the sun's arrows. The Oak was the last of her kind, alone in second-growth, third-growth forests. A shame. I saluted her and went on my way.

Atop Sinking Creek Mountain, the Trail emerged from the trees and onto slabs of rock, which echoed the sun's heat. I needed a siesta and a splash of water. My clothes were sopping with sweat. I parked myself on a shaded rock, where a lizard scuttled away. Ten seconds after I sat, I heard something clattering on the rocks about twenty yards up the Trail. I leaned forward to look. Something peeked back at me from behind a boulder. A goat! Before I could fetch my camera, three goats were licking my legs, as if they were the last source of salt on Earth. I could hardly move, being tongue-tied by three spastic billies. My efforts to pet them were dodged, unless I offered my arms as a sacrifice. They slimed them, too.

If goat spit is as healing as a dog's is supposed to be, these guys could work wonders on cuts and scrapes, I thought.

When I stood to leave, the goats fought for my rocky seat, licking it with passion. My departure wasn't made in secret, though. Within two shakes of a goat's tail, they were on my heels, making sure they got all they could of me. Slimy goat tongues slithered across my calves, my thighs, and my hands. I pulled my shorts out of one goat's mouth and scampered away. Who knew what I smelled like after that rendezvous?

Too bad I don't have any of Apple's tooth-numbing crème for the goat's amusement, I thought. *Then again, maybe these goats can help Apple's toothache.*

Trail Tidbit #36
Slightly Ticked Off

Journal Entry
6/20/00 - From John's Hollow Shelter to Brown Mountain Creek Shelter (17.6 miles)

I always hate a steep climb first thing in the morning, but I managed well because of gentle temperatures. A small stone memorial on top of Bluff Mountain marked where five-year-old Little Ottie Cline Powell died in 1891. According to my Trail Companion, his schoolteacher had sent him out to gather firewood. He got lost. His body was found dead, seven miles away from school, on Bluff Mountain.

I wondered about that little boy. Did he see the same things I saw today? What about those long stone walls built by freed slaves to clear space for sharecropping? Maybe he followed them, too. Perhaps he knew some of its builders.

Mad Dog was at the shelter with his usual fire, when Apple and I arrived. B&B followed. Good to see them again. Trail Angels Flash and his wife Hot Flash greeted us with cold Pepsi. They're members of the Potomac Appalachian Trail Club and Natural Bridge Appalachian Trail Club.

Now I am sprawled out in my tent, writing in this journal. My flashlight's dead, but Mad Dog's fire glows bright enough to scribble by. Moments ago, Apple cried out from his tent, "I found a tick!"

"You're kidding!" I said. "I better check myself!" Frantically, I smoothed my hands over every inch of my body, afraid of what I might find.

"I think I found one! Can you bring your flashlight? Hurry!"

Apple darted over in his skivvies. Sure enough, a critter was boring into my side. Incredulous. There it was—the sneaky, revolting, leech! How dare it!

"Don't pull it off," Apple whispered. "They say its head will break off into your skin and get infected."

"I'll get my tick remover," I said. I performed the minor surgery without hesitation.

"Check my back," Apple said.

"Clear. Check mine," I said.

"Nothing."

Whew!

Feeling vandalized and victimized, we decided that the ticks must pay for this monumental offense—either forty lashes with the bottom of my sandal, or burning at the stake in the fire pit. But we flicked them into the woods instead. I returned to my tent with caution. Paranoid, I dissected my sleeping bag and gear in search of more invaders.

So, here I lie, squinting to see the page, twitching at every itch and prickle, as if I had a nervous tick, to make sure it's not another bug. Tomorrow is Hike Naked Day... I'm wearing armor.

Trail Tidbit #37
The Naked Truth

ummer Solstice was the annual Hike Naked Day. The phrase "Are you going to hike nude?" visited every dialogue the week before the holiday. I'm not sure what was more exciting: the anticipation of seeing who dared to do it, or the actualization. At least, during the suspense, you could *imagine* whom first and risk disappointment later. But when the Day arrives, you were more apt to be *disappointed* first and be left only to imagine whom later—depending upon whom you were with, I guess.

"What about you, Small World? Will we see you hiking naked tomorrow?" asked Beth (of B&B).

"No way!" I said. "You gotta be joking."

"Come on!" B&B goaded, as if it were my turn at bat; my chance to hit a homer.

"Sorry to disappoint you," I replied, "but dis boy don't swing like dat!"

I was first out of camp, making my escape fully clad. Mad Dog and B&B still snoozed in the shelter. Good. That way they'd never know for sure, whether or not I stripped. It was a muggy morning, perfect day to go buff-blazing. But no. Not I. Foul ball. Think again.

Two miles later, I rested at a picnic table where the Trail crossed VA 60. Moments later, Apple howled from the other side of the road behind me.

"Wahoo!" he crowed, like a victorious warrior. I spun around to see a little white rump retreating into the woods as a car raced by. Apple came out with his pants up and a gloating smile. I thanked him for dressing.

"I won't hike with a naked man," I said. "Including myself!"

At the top of the second inning, I called another time-out. The mountaintop was bald, so the sun scorched the grassy field, where we sat under a stray tree. Suddenly, not one, not two, not even three—but *thirty* girls frolicked by. They didn't see us. But they were fully clothed.

"Hey, don't y'all know it's Hike Naked Day?" we longed to ask.

"We're such hypocrites," Apple said.

"Yeah, I guess we can't expect them to honor the holiday, which we ourselves are not celebrating," I replied.

Cool Hand Luke and Fennel were merrily hopping along, when they were caught with their pants down by the Thirtysomething. They hid behind a bush. When they had gathered their wits, they casually mingled into the crowd, as if hiking naked were an everyday affair. Poor girls.

Perhaps I did miss my turn at bat. With the bases loaded, I may have scored big. *Nah!* There were others to whom I left that challenge: those with better conditioning and confidence at the plate. I just figured, *If you don't play, you can't strike out. Perhaps I'm a poor sport. But at least I'm a modest poor sport!*

Trail Tidbit #38
Accessorized

eorgia... North Carolina... Tennessee... and now halfway through Virginia. I began in Georgia as a novice backpacker, but I had surely *looked* as if I knew what I was doing. My equipment was well-researched, top-shelf stuff. Only keen eyes could have told that I was a beginner by noticing that everything I owned was sparkling new. But I also had practiced how to use my gear before coming to the Trail. Not everyone did that. Eve didn't.

I delved into a bag of GORP for a midmorning snack. The shelter was packed with other snackers, late sleepers, and newcomers to the AT. Eve was the latter type. She was fixing herself breakfast, fiddling at length with her stove.

"Shoot! Does anyone know how to light this thing?"

Hum-de-dum-dee-dum.... No one "heard" her. No one spoke.

"Darnit! I guess I'll have to eat another bowl of cold oatmeal," she said.

Guess so. How could you start the Trail without basic operating knowledge of your gear?

Gear was the Beauty *and* the Beast of backpacking. Some of it I loved, and some of it I hated loving. By the Middle Miles, my Lowe Alpine backpack weighed less than forty pounds. I had executed several of its inmates. Accessories. It had started at fifty pounds, but compared to some packs, even *that* was something to put on airs about.

Amos, whom I met on the bus to Gainesville, Georgia, clocked in at sixty-five pounds. He carried a guitar and a machete. We called him Gonzo, like the Muppet. I understood the guitar, but what did the machete have to do with Gonzo the Muppet? His performing chickens? Gonzo the Hiker's knees went bankrupt and closed after just three weeks in business. His store had too much cache.

The official AT maps were lighter than machetes but not any more necessary. If someone needed a machete to cut through the Trail, or a map to find his way, then he wasn't on the AT. Nonetheless, the maps diagramed the Trail's elevation profile, which was handy for strategizing daily distances. They were extras, luxury items.

The maps revealed that weeks of easy terrain were ahead of us through the Shenandoah National Park. It was a good time to lighten up and de-accessorize, in order to pile on miles. Apple and I tried on new boots in Waynesboro, Virginia.

"One pound on the foot is five on the back," Apple reminded me.

"How about these trail-shoes?" I said. "They're three times lighter than my boots." I felt like a kid with new shoes, who imagined he could now run faster. But this was for real. I would be super swift... had I been under less pressure—my pack was plainly too heavy. I brought all my gear into the store to test it in a new backpack. My Lowe Alpine sat in a corner, while I stuffed each item into the new, lighter Kelty.

"How much money do you want for your Lowe?" asked a stranger. He was on the same mission as I. "Hi, I'm Grumpy, and this is my wife Snow White. Wanna sell your pack to me? I need a better one." I looked at my green pack and played with a few dollar signs.

Thirty pieces of silver, I thought, *to betray a friend...*

I had climbed Springer with that pack. I had stomped through rain, snow, sun, hail, mud, meadows, and three months with that pack. I had sweat gallons in that pack.

"I'm sorry, it's not for sale." I said. My backpack was priceless. Besides, it was still a better pack than the one I was buying—more rugged and suitable for the later months. So, my original backpack went home; a companion I promised to reunite with at a later date.

Another friend that I had to part with that day was Apple. He had already completed much of the Shenandoahs earlier in the year. From Waynesboro, he was hitching forward. I was sorry to see him go. I had climbed so many peaks with him. I had weathered many days and got grubby with him.

"We'll meet up again," he said. "I'll be taking a week off with my wife, and I have a wedding to go to. That'll give you time to catch up. I'll leave notes in the shelter registers for you."

Apple rode away in a car.

Again, I was on my own.

New backpack. New shoes. Accessories. Some of them I loved, some of them I hated loving. But friends were like luxury items I loved having. I hoped I would see Apple again.

Above: One of the best things about walking through meadows during the day's infancy was the chance actually to see the sun sit up in its cradle and smile at me.

Below: Rusty was a Vietnam War veteran, who opened up his electricity-free home to hikers. His biggest concern was that every hiker look after his or her brother. We didn't dare eat our blueberry pancakes at dinnertime if we knew that other hikers were yet to arrive.

Trail Tidbit #39
Technology of Acceptance

T wo new shoes plus one lighter backpack equals three quicker paces. Enter the Shenandoah National Park. A kiosk alongside the Trail was stuffed with mandatory backcountry permits. I scribbled my name and address. Date: June 26. Location of entry: Rockfish Gap. Location of exit: Front Royal, Virginia. Number of people in group: one. Just me. Apple was long gone.

I liked the idea of going solo for a while again. I felt rugged and gruff. No one knew where I was. I was alive and strong, making my way north, while the rest of the world did its little thing, oblivious to and careless of my existence. I was happy.

Tree's voice crept through the woods like a barbecue grill's fragrance roaming the neighborhood. *In a sense,* Tree whispered, *you've been wandering alone for years now.*

"Hello to you, too," I said. "Yes, I have been wandering. I guess I've been discontent in life. I just don't jive with that 'Bigger, Better, Faster' mentality: 'I gotta upgrade my computer. I gotta trade in my car. I gotta move away. I gotta gotta gotta.' Yet, I run after these things, as if life would leave me behind if I didn't keep up with the technology."

Do you have a problem with the developing technology?

"Sometimes I think I do," I said. "I'm not sure why. Maybe I *should* embrace it; it's the way of the world."

There is no should or shouldn't about embracing the technological race today. It's not an issue of right or wrong. Remember, the question is, Does it work?

"Sometimes I feel as if it eats my soul," I said.

Don't let it, Tree said. *Technology is only applied knowledge, Small World. Humans have been using it for millions of years and teaching it to their young. Even chimpanzees will stick a twig in a termite hole to catch a treat. That's technology. Stone-age tribes don't get down on themselves for their technology, which is much more advanced than the chimp's.*

"Then what is it, Tree? Why do I feel so abandoned in the world? My parents were good to me. They even taught me everything they knew about God and the life he was supposed to offer."

A red bird landed on one of Tree's arms. *There's a lot of mix-up between life and religion,* Tree said. *Religion is a tool; is Life a tool? If you remember, I told you that if the hammer is broken, then don't fix things with it.*

"I remember," I said. "Were you suggesting that the church is broken?"

Not exactly, said Tree. *You told me that religion didn't work well for you. I suggested that if your tool to find purpose and meaning wasn't working for you, then don't keep using it. Find the right tool for the job.*

"I get it now. And I'd told you that the AT had become my tool," I said.

Tree's upper twigs nodded. *This is your vision quest. Your walkabout. Your rite of passage.*

"If I were Jewish, then maybe it would be my proverbial bar mitzvah."

Very insightful, said Tree. *The AT is your coming-of-age ritual—a practice your culture sees less and less of.*

"It seems that the more we see of technology, the less we see of ourselves," I said.

It's a double-edged sword. Technology brings people together, decreasing the distances between them; yet it also gives you reason to stay home if you can just pick up the phone. But applied knowledge is not at fault for devouring your soul. Whose fault is it?

"My own?"

Why?

"Because I make the technology?"

Don't be ridiculous, said Tree. *It's not because you make technology that you feel consumed. Nor is it why you see less of your humanity. Rather, it's because you're preoccupied by it. It's that 'Bigger, Better, Faster' mentality that you talked about. It's the belief that you* must *embrace it. And while you're preoccupied finding pseudo-*

security and pseudo-power and pseudo-control and pseudo-freedom, you forget about finding yourselves. A few of you, however, gather the courage to walk away.

"That's what I did," I said.

You stepped outside the box, giving yourself room to grow. The preoccupation with "Bigger, Better, Faster" wasn't working for you. A preoccupation with anything can destroy your true self. Including religion. Religion is one of many tools in life, but is not life-giving itself.

"Jesus said that he came to give us life, but I've been striving for years to experience it, feeling empty."

Why have you felt empty?

"Lack of community?"

Don't tell me what you think I want to hear, Small World. You've had community your whole life. Perhaps what's closer to the truth is you've been unable to find your place in those communities. Why do you think that is?

"Because I don't always believe my beliefs, and I don't always believe in myself."

Ouch, Tree said with a shake of a branch.

"Yeah, ouch," I said.

Isn't that what it comes down to? You don't accept yourself. Why not?

I hesitated. I wished I could cry, but I'd forgotten how. "I don't know what to believe about myself, partly because I don't accept everything I see or hear. Not even from you, Tree."

You've spent your life deciding Who and What you are. Yet you still don't know.

I bowed my head. "Not really. And if it were presented to me, then I couldn't guarantee that I'd accept it."

That's why it won't be presented to you. You must find it yourself.

"How do I begin?

You've already begun. Before you find out what *you are, however, it may be helpful to think about the fact* that *you are.*

"*That* I am?"

Stop hiking for a moment, said Tree. *Good. Now look at me. Choose any tree.*

I stepped off the Trail and found a tree a hundred yards away.

Sit, relax, and take a hard look at me.

Propped up against my backpack, I stared at a tree for twenty minutes. The tree's lichen-speckled trunk bolted straight upwards, as if having been shot from deep underground by a flare gun. It exploded high above into a mushroom cloud of bright green leaves. It staggered my mind.

You are the first person to look at this tree in this way, said Tree. *Truthfully, you're the only person who knows it exists at all.*

"Oh, I'm sorry," I said.

Don't be, said Tree. *Most of life on Earth exists without mankind's knowing it. And to be frank, we're better off for it. The next person to see me may have a chainsaw in his hand. But I may get to sit here for another two hundred years. In that time, I may never be seen by another human, but I'll be thriving and happy nonetheless.*

You see, Small World, in my own way I know I exist. And I exist apart from anyone's knowledge of my existence. Most of the universe exists without your knowing it. Humans don't give it purpose and reason to exist. If all of you disappeared, the stars and galaxies would go on without you.

You exist in much this same way. You are alone on the Trail right now and most of the world has no idea that you exist. Those that know you don't even know where you are. But you still go on. You exist, Small World, and to know that you exist is a miracle itself.

"I feel so small," I said.

You are. But you exist. Think about that. *It may help you discover* what *you* are.

I chewed on these ideas with a Snickers bar. I came to realize that I have never accepted my simple existence and expected that no one else did, either.

You are the only shot this universe has at expressing itself as you!

"And I am alive," I said to myself. "How amazing."

The Appalachian Trail was the tool that helped me to realize I was alive. It took my being alive to heave my backpack onto my shoulders. It took my being alive to clamber up and down the mountains. It took my being alive to find water, to taste food, to build a fire, to make friends. It took my being alive to see, hear, touch, and smell beauty. And when I finish the Trail, I would still exist to do all these things in everyday life. I could accept that.

Trail Tidbit #40
Ursa Major

Notice
WARNING!

Posted on the tree in front of me, a laminated page read: "Bear problems between Milam Gap and Big Meadows."

"Oh, boy," I said to myself... since I was alone. I was at Milam Gap. I memorized the list of rules to follow, in case I met a bear. Then I crept forward, eyes peeled.

The setting was movie-perfect. Dense fog rolled in like concert smoke. The forest was noiseless—haunted maybe. I could imagine the sneak preview: Mad Maullie, the true story of the evil man-eating black bear of the Blue Ridge Mountains. The mists blended my vision with my imagination. Every boulder and bush was a bear.

Oh, shi— no, wait... That's another shrub.

Caution lead the way forward. Tiptoes.

"Don't look her in the eyes. Back away slowly," I recited. It was too quiet.

At least I'll hear her coming.

"Don't run. Keep your backpack in place," I continued. The rocky cliffs to my right looked just like those at a zoo, where bears were kept.

My imagination brought me back to the Smokies.

A poor lady was killed by a bear in the Great Smokies just two weeks after I was there, I mused. Surely that same bear was the troublemaker here—the Appalachian ridge-runner, hunting for gullible hikers. Soon my confidence picked up with my pace. I figured that if I hadn't been attacked thus far, I must be safe.

FWOOSH! pressed my panic button.

A bear pounced into my imagination, and I twirled around to face my accuser. Good golly, Miss Maullie!

Fwoosh, fwoosh, fwoosh....

"Oh." It was not a bear. It was a vulture, departing its rotting carcass meal with morbid morsels of flesh plummeting to the earth from its beak.

Still, I thought, I don't need the smell of fresh flesh and blood to fill the air to attract Mad Maullie to me.

I lost all poise and cranked up the speed. Needless to say, I made it. There would be safety in numbers at Big Meadows Wayside Campground.

The more people there are, the more people to eat, I thought. Miss Maullie shall never notice my leaving in the morning.

The Buck Stops Here

Seventeen dollars? *That's nuts!* There was no way I was going to fork over that much money to take a snooze. This called for stealth-camping (as in sneak-camping, not klepto-camping). Stealth-camping was what one did, when a campsite was not to be found via a shelter or otherwise. In the boonies or in parks, being stealthy was often necessary, because campsites weren't always there, when I was ready for dinner and bed, and prices at park campgrounds were ridiculously high for my limited means. I refused to pay them. I had a budget to keep to get me to Katahdin.

Under cover of darkness, I would pitch my tent behind some trees, but first, I needed a shower. The weather was unseasonably cold and wet. I was caked with days of sweat, grime, stench, and chill. *Oh, a hot shower to dissolve all my problems....*

"Two dollars," said the bathroom maid.

"For what?" I asked.

"The showers are coin operated. Two dollars."

"Two bucks? For how long?"

"Five minutes," she replied.

"What?" I blurted, "That's absurd!"

"Well, it can be done if you set all your stuff out on the bench, see."

"Look, I've been hiking all day—all week. It'll take me five minutes just to do my hair."

"Not my problem," she said.

Bitch, I thought. "I've gone longer without a shower before… I think I'll pass!" I said. In all honesty, I sort of regretted it. Seriously, two dollars is not that much. Neither is five minutes. But I'd just bought new shoes and backpack, so my budget was especially tight, and I didn't feel like being exploited. Tired and irked, I huffed off, and found a secret place for my tent among some trees, heavy fog, and darkness.

These eastern mountains seem to be enshrouded with exploitation, since the founding of America. Kick out the Natives; these mountains have money in them! Virgin forests? To hell with them—look at the board feet of lumber! Outdoor enthusiasts? Screw 'em! They'll come in droves with their pockets full of cash…

I wouldn't let them mine me for silver, until Maine was in my pocket. Maine was months away, and if I had to wait until then to bathe in a tub, I would.

Trial Tidbit #42
The Park Shark

wenty-six miles would be my farthest hike in one day without slack-packing. And it felt good.

Are the Shenandoahs easy, or am I in good shape? I thought. *Both maybe.*

The Zone dialed the focus wheel, and the Trail blurred underneath my feet. My imagination sharpened, and I saw Tree standing all around me: many different trees, all one Tree. It was as if I could feel Tree's spirit. But I didn't dare listen for its voice. I wasn't ready for that again. Too mind boggling atop weary feet. Silence was good, too.

I wondered about Apple: what he was doing; where he was hiking.

"I bet all that's on his mind, is his wife," I said to myself. "Mine would be, too."

My thoughts lingered on, and I dreamed about what it would be like to be married. *Will I ever have a woman to wrap my love around?* I longed for that personal touch. *Or will I always be alone?* I have always enjoyed being alone, too. Especially on the Trail. But besides missing a woman, I missed Apple.

"Small World! Is it really you?" someone hollered.

I turned around. "Scottish John! Lynda!" I cheered. "It's so good to see you two again. It's been weeks since I last saw you!"

"Aye," said Scottish John.

I had met Scottish John and Lynda at Elmer's—the Inn in Hot Springs, North Carolina—where we had sat on the balcony late into the night, reading excerpts from Bill Bryson's hilarious book *A Walk in the Woods.*

"Good to see you're still on the Trail," I said.

"Likewise," said Lynda.

"This calls for a celebration," said Scottish John. "Let's get some more miles in before dark and have dinner together at camp."

I was never alone on the Trail for very long: a blessing and a curse.

Nighttime sneaked into the treetops, slid down their trunks, and burrowed into the ferns.

"Where are we going to camp?" Lynda asked.

"Well, according to the Data Book, we should be close to Elkwallow Gap, next to the Blue Ridge Parkway," I said. "That must be another one of those roadside parks."

"I don't believe it is permitted to overnight at the parks," Scottish John replied.

"We don't have much choice," I said. "It's dark, and I don't know where else to go. We'll just wake up early and leave before anyone sees us."

Flush toilets. Tap water. Picnic tables. Soft grass. How nice. Sound sleep. All night. Alarm beep. Six o'clock. Blink blink. Stretch stretch. Oh, yes... must leave.

I bumbled out of my tent. Scottish John and Lynda were already tearing theirs down. Willy-nilly, I yanked out my stakes.

Pop-Tarts today, or oatmeal? I pondered.

"Um, Small World? Look here, please," Scottish John called.

I peeped up, and by-golly if it wasn't a car with flashing lights on its roof! The door opened. A booted foot dropped down to the ground with a thud. A valiant park ranger hopped out of the chariot, decked in full armor: bulletproof vest, badge, sunglasses, Batman belt with sidearm and cuffs. This guy was serious and wanted to be taken seriously. But I couldn't imagine little minnows, like us, being of any danger. So, why the weapons? Sharks didn't need teeth to eat minnows, did they? I had my eye on his gun. Perhaps sharks flashed their teeth to remind everyone who was a shark and who was a minnow. We three minnows looked at the shark and gulped.

"Do you realize you're not allowed to camp here?" he asked, pointing at the No Camping sign next to the Trail.

"Uh, no," we answered in unison. "We got here after dark. Musta missed the sign."

"I need some IDs and Park passes," said the ranger.

Oh, great, I thought, *John's gonna get deported.*

The Park Shark then sat in his car and made sure we weren't criminal minnows. He issued us warnings—in effect for three years.

"Next time will be a ticket," he said then turned about-fin and zoomed away. He had other reefs to hunt. We gobbled our fish-food and moved upstream.

Trail Tidbit #43
The Flukey Fourth

19.3 miles, 22.1 miles, 20.4 miles, 26 miles, 19.2 miles, 15.1 miles, 18 miles, 20.7 miles.

"1000 miles!" I cheered, as I passed the 1000-mile marker, coming into Harpers Ferry, West Virginia. "And sixteen percent of that done just since last Monday!"

It wasn't just the new shoes and lighter pack; it was the gentle terrain, weeks of conditioning, and hopes of catching Apple. His notes in shelter registers had ceased. Maybe I would see him in Harpers Ferry.

Tomorrow's Independence Day. I'm taking a zero day.

I shared into a cheap hotel room on the outskirts of Harpers Ferry—*Ah, a hot shower... finally*—where the Appalachian Trail Conference is headquartered (now called the Appalachian Trail Conservancy). A sign on the front door of the ATC told hikers to feel free to bring in their packs. I left mine on the porch; it was nice not to have to carry it around for a bit, while the ATC director, Laurie Potteiger, gave me a tour. I reverently touched the original wooden Katahdin summit sign. Laurie took my polaroids, and I signed and added it to the album. The ATC staff shook my hand, congratulated me, and wished me well to Maine.

I phoned a friend the next chance I got. Almost one year ago, I had helped her move to a new house in Frederick, Maryland, near where the Trail crosses I-70 on a footbridge. It had been a long drive from the Chicago suburbs, and I had been getting sleepy at the wheel. But when I saw that footbridge over the road with a sign on it that read "Appalachian Trail." I had nearly wrecked the car at my first glimpse of the Trail. Now I was thrilled to be back.

"Hey, Jamie! I'm in Harpers Ferry," I said.

"Wow! You made it this far already?" she replied.

"Already?" I laughed. "I'd like to see you and your husband. You doing anything on the Fourth?"

"This is perfect!" Jamie squealed. "My sister just flew in from Chicago for the Holiday. We were planning on going to Harpers Ferry tomorrow!"

"Paula's here, too? Fantastic! What a coincidence" I said.

"Yeah, small world, huh?" Jamie replied.

"You have no idea," I said. It was this kind of Trail Magic that gave an extra boost when needed.

Jamie and Paula were shocked to see the new me: hairy, thin, and smelly. They pretended not to notice the stench, but congratulated my makeover. We spent the day in old-town Harpers Ferry, West Virginia, exploring the museums, ruins, the ATC Headquarters, and frozen custard shops.

"We'll see you when you get to the I-70 footbridge," Paula said.

"Yes!" I said. "Give me a couple days."

"Two days? That's a long way for two days," Jamie said.

"It's only twenty-two miles by foot. That's nothing," I replied.

After the weekend in Frederick, I was less hairy, more heavy, and less smelly. I cut my scraggly beard down to a goatee, had several good meals and a stocked backpack, and several hot showers. We each went our merry ways: I hit the Trail, Jamie went back to her job, and Paula returned to the 'burbs to inform all of our friends, "I had a Welchie sighting!" I'd had a sighting, too: a vision of carrots everywhere in my virtual carrot patch of success. With my pack reloaded on my back, my hat on my head, nearly half of the AT under my belt, and the world on my side, I was bound for Maine.

Top Left: On a peak over Maryland stands the first monument for George Washington, built 1827.

Top Right: I was suspended over I-70, awaiting my flukey freaky friends from Frederick, MD. I hoped they would recognize me—now thinner and shaggier.

Bottom: Emily, Jamie, and Paula DID recognize me!

Trail Tidbit #44
Milestones

Journal Entry
7/11/00 - From Pine Grove Furnace State Park to Boiling Springs, PA (19 miles)

Goodbye South. Hello North! I've been on a high ever since I stepped into Pennsylvania from Maryland across the Mason-Dixon Line—the historical dividing border between South and North; Slave and Free. The Middle Miles are behind me. And the Virginia Blues? What a horrible perspective of the Trail. There's so much to experience in Virginia. The only Blues I whistled were the Blue Ridge Mountains and the Blue Ridge Parkway.

Sure, I admit that I didn't always like it; there weren't always "rewards" around every bend. But then again, that's just wishy-washy sensationalism. When I look at my AT experience from my non-Trail eyes, then the Trail becomes a Rat Race to get to the next big thing—the next reward. On the other hand, when I look at the AT as my life now, then the Trail *is* the reward. Life here is rewarding in itself. A Tree taught me that.

This doesn't make hiking the Trail easy, however. Each day must be taken one step at a time. Yet, I can't help but notice how little coincidences keep pulling me forward. I don't see them as a "reward." They're more like a motivational device. They're always occurring, and when I recognize them, they seem to spur me onward. For example, I crossed the official Halfway Mark today on 7/11. I have always thought of Seven-Eleven as a lucky mix of numbers. It just feels right. It sounds like a jackpot. (I think there's a lottery ticket called 7-11.)

Just past the Halfway Mark, I heard somebody singing. Somewhere ahead of me, a voice rang out in Disney fashion, "It's a small world after all. It's a small world after all..." I ignored it, never putting two and two together (arithmetic has never been my strongest subject). It was Apple! After two weeks, there he was! Talk about coincidence!

"Why are you going south?" I asked.

"After spending a few days with my wife in New York, it just made more sense to hike south from there," he said. "When I get to Harper's Ferry, I'll get a ride back up north, and meet my brother Bob. You can take a zero day with me at his house in Doylestown, PA."

"...If we're lucky enough to meet again," I said.

We planned on a date that I need to arrive in Delaware Water Gap. If I did 160 miles in eight days, through the Shenandoahs, can I do 170 miles to get there in time? I'm not so sure... not with these rocks! The horror stories are true: "Pennsylvania is where your boots go to die!"

Twisting, turning, and wrenching my feet, I traversed several miles today, without even touching bare ground. Each step was carefully placed on stone, rock or boulder. I hardly remember any views or scenic overlooks today—with my gaze so trained on the Trail. "Can't see the forest for the rocks." It's quite a rock concert, as Apple would have said.

Camp is filled with the moans and whimpers of frustrated hikers with aching ankles and arches. *When does it end?* Aw, not to complain too much... but it feels good to whine sometimes. "A little for what ails you," they say, right? Statistics confirm, that a little whine each day is good for the circulation. OK, ok. Enough with the dry whine humor. But a good sense of humor does help to get through these rocky times: "a little *cheese* with my whine." How about some "whine—on the rocks," please?

Trail Tidbit #45
Encore, Encore!

"Y ou lived in a Trappist monastery?" I asked.

"Yeah, for a month," said Hilltopper. "Right before hitting the Trail a couple of weeks ago."

"Oh, so you're a section-hiker?" I asked. Hilltopper was a new face on the Trail.

"Nope. I'm on my way to Maine from Harpers Ferry and will be returning there to hike back to Springer in the Fall."

"A flip-flop," I said.

"Exactly."

Trappists are a Catholic order of monks who, among other things, vow to silence.

Boy, I thought, *you really gotta be serious to spend a whole month in a Trappist monastery. Seriously religious.* It wasn't something I would do. Sounded spooky: a bunch of robed men, mulling, skulking around like the Grim Reaper. *Hear no evil, speak no evil, see no evil.* More like *make no sound, speak no word, and keep out of sight,* in order to survive. Out of sight, out of mind. But just because you couldn't see them, didn't mean they weren't there. Spooky.

No-see-ums were an exception to the out-of-sight-out-of-mind rule.

They forced me into my tent that evening. *Zip!* Goodbye flies. Hello dreamland. *Ah, to sleep the night away....*

Huh? What? Who the—— It's not even six in the morning!
Hilltopper was singing at the top of his lungs.
He's gone mad, I thought.
I rolled over. *It's too early.*
Then he began crooning hymns.
Oh, God! I prayed.
"Small World!" he called. "Are you still alive?"
"No," I bellowed.
"I'll be over in a minute to tell you why I'm singing!"
Lovely, I thought, *Hilltopper must have just reached Enlightenment.*
There was no use trying to sleep now. Hilltopper was on his way to preach the Good News. I bumbled out of my tent and started gearing up. Moments later, Hilltopper bolted over to me, packed and ready to hike.
"I was laying in my tent, right?" he said. "All of a sudden, I heard this sniffing around outside. Oh, Man! I started praying, 'Lord, let that be a really big opossum!' I heard it walk around my tent and stop several yards away from the front of my tent. I figured, 'What the heck,' so I peeked out under the rainfly and saw two bears standing on their hind legs, pawing each other!"
"You're kidding," I said. "I didn't even hear anything."
"I started singing to scare them away."
"It must have worked."
"Yeah, but I guess I need to work on my songs a bit."
Just because you couldn't see them, didn't mean they weren't there, I thought. *Spooky.*
They may have sniffed around my tent, too—like Grim Reapers—while I slept, out of sight. If it weren't for Hilltopper's singing, I could have been trapped, ravaged! Thank God Hilltopper hadn't taken that vow of silence. We both could have been Trappists forever: goodbye life, hello Grim Reaper.
"You can sing all you want, Hilltopper," I said.

One Fine Chick

Stretched between two Pennsylvanian mountain ranges lay the Cumberland Valley: fifteen blissful, flat miles of golden hay and emerald corn stalks. Because no camping was allowed anywhere on that stretch of farmland, many hikers stayed with Mother Hen in Boiling Springs.

Like a true mama bird, she watched over us, tending to our every need, until we hatched free, full of life and vitality. Her nest was open to everyone for as long as necessary. Sixteen people ambled in and out of her kitchen, shower and living room. It was a cuckoo's nest, but Mother Hen kept her cool, cooking huge meals, and making her coop a warm place to be.

I relaxed on her living room couch with a book I'd found on her bookshelf. The first chapter sucked me in, as the characters talked about a sense of restlessness and preoccupation in their lives. *Hm, that sounds familiar,* I thought. They also noticed how uncanny coincidences seemed to pull their lives forward. *Hm, I can relate to that, too.* According to the book, coincidences should be watched for and listened to for their lessons and directions. They were *more* than coincidences.

"Wow, Mother Hen, this is intriguing," I said.

"Isn't it?" she replied. "Take the book with you. For some reason, I have two of them on the shelf."

"What a coincidence," I said. "People have been telling me to read this book. Thank you."

I stuffed *The Celestine Prophecy* into my backpack. Its paper leafs would emit the voice of Tree, suggesting new ideas to consider, including the mysteriousness of unexplainable coincidences. Was it more than a coincidence that Mother Hen had two of this book on her shelf?

"Mother Hen, do you really believe that coincidences are more than what they seem, as if something or someone were behind them?"

"Well, I don't know exactly what's behind them, but it's fun to watch happen. Fun to experience," she said.

"True enough," I said. "Trail magic happens all the time. Even my trailname was born out of a coincidence. But come on… Is there a cosmic meaning behind my being named 'Small World?' Was it *meant* to be? Or is it all just spiritual candy with no particular purpose?"

"That could be, too," said Mother Hen, "but it is fun to step outside the box and wonder. It could all be a load of crap, but it makes life adventuresome to experience it. I mean, *what if* coincidence signifies Providence?"

I sank into her couch. Perplexed. Intrigued. Bewildered.

Mother Hen shook a Tupperware of marinated chicken.

Hikers ducked in and out of the Hen-house.

"Mother Hen," I said. "If coincidences were *meant* to happen, then doesn't that imply that a Higher Power *intended* for them to happen?"

Mother Hen dipped her finger in the marinade. "Seems so." She sucked on her fingertip. "But what that Higher Power is… is rather mysterious. Is it a conscious Force? If so, is its consciousness independent of us? Could it be a collective consciousness, like Dr. Jung talked about? You know, Small World, some people call it Source, or Oneness, or The Force, Spirit, or even God…"

I cringed.

Mother Hen tilted her head. "Sweetheart, do you have something against God?"

"God… God. I guess I have a hard time accepting that 'coincidences' are proof that such an deity exists."

"Deity?" said Mother Hen. "Why must it be a deity—a 'spiritual *thing*' that is somehow *out there?* Worldwide, people experience the Divine in ways that are nothing like a deity or even a conscious being meddling in our lives. Rather, it's energetic. It's spirit. It's experiential. I bet you've experienced what I mean on the AT. At least a little."

"My empirical inclinations dumped me into agnosticism by now," I said, the first time I'd ever said it aloud. "If God exists, but he cannot observed and measured, then what use is there being a God, since we experience our world through our senses?"

Mother Hen replied, "If there is a God, yet he cannot be proved with any of our five senses, then what use are our senses?"

"Useful senses don't prove God," I said.

"No, I mean it. I'm agreeing with you, but seriously... what use are our senses?"

I tried not to sound rude. "Obviously, to see, hear, taste, smell, and touch."

"Exactly. To experience," she said.

I said, "So?"

"So, perhaps the experience itself is the Divine."

"Huh?" I said.

"Small World, when you lick an ice cream cone after a long week of hiking, what do you sense? Obviously, the ice cream cone is not God; nor is your tongue; nor is the act of licking. What do you experience?"

"Pleasure. Joy. Thankfulness. Fun. Enrichment..." I said.

"Believe me," said Mother Hen, "that's fairly universal. Perhaps that's God—the essence, the energy, the spirit, the experience of life, which you get a taste of with that ice cream. Maybe God is that very *Existence*."

"Hmm. The I Am-ness," I said. "Then if God is the immeasurable experience of our sensations, then no wonder people like me become agnostic."

Mother Hen ruffled her apron. "Quite possible, Small World, if you expect God to be measurable But all along God has been right in front of our noses, eyes, mouths, ears, and hands."

I replied, "Or perhaps more to your point, God is in our noses, eyes, mou—"

"Right on, Small World! In the experience. In the essence itself."

"What about negative experiences?" I asked.

"No denying them," said Mother Hen. "But isn't it sadness that makes happiness so happy? Joy is what we thrive on and find life through; but it's so joyful because we know sorrow, too. God is in the experience of both."

Whatever, whoever God is, I knew that my former dogmatic approach had allowed me to become stale, rather than to evolve spiritually. It seemed that coincidences indeed happened all the time—it's a small world, after all. And experiencing those coincidences felt as magical and serendipitous as peeking over the lid of a mountain to see what was inside its valleys. And I wanted more.

Top Left: Corn and hay filled Pennsylvania's Cumberland Valley, allowing no shade trees under the blazing sun. I preferred getting roasted than hiking one step farther on the Pennsylvanian rocks!

Bottom Left: I was amazed to see Nails, Fenway, Dammit and Purple at Windsor Furnace shelter, scouting out the terrain through a map. I hadn't seen them since Damascus!

Top Left: At least to the right of PA's Knife Edge was a fantastic view over a cultivated valley.

Trail Tidbit #47
Roadblock to Advancement

Journal Entry

7/19/00—From Windsor Furnace Shelter to Eckville Shelter (9.1 miles)

Rain again. Why? Please! I stopped at Eckville Shelter to wait out the rainy cold summer day. I actually had intentions of hiking farther, but when the rain stopped, I was so enjoying my new book, that I stayed. Besides, the shelter is fully enclosed with a table and bunks. It's a converted shed, which sits behind the caretaker's (Lazee) house. Outside Lazee's house is a hiker fridge with Gatorade, Pepsi, ice-cream sandwiches, and juice for a donation. Lazee said that today's temperatures were record summer lows.

Roadblock, a section-hiker, is here with me. I couldn't concentrate to read, because he was munching Peanut M&Ms like a camel—mouth smacking and teeth clicking. I could hardly believe he didn't startle himself. My nerves began to unwind, and I wanted to cover my ears with a pillow. For some reason I find myself not liking him. It's not that we don't get along... we just have no desire to talk to each other. I even find myself glaring at him sometimes. I don't like that—don't know why I do it. It's irrational.

7/20/00—From Eckville Shelter to George W. Outerbridge Shelter (24.2 miles)

A golden sunrise. Splotchy pink and blue wisps. Drab gray rocks. Rocks. Rocks. Boulders galore! Stone salad! At least it wasn't raining. That makes all the difference in the world to me. There was a stretch of blueberries on both sides of the Trail just before Lehigh Gap. Blueberry fields forever! They were the juiciest, most flavorful blueberries I've seen yet.

While hiking, my thoughts wandered through the pages of my book. My reflections lead look at Roadblock again. What was my beef with him? Why do I act so aloof towards him? Shouldn't I give him a chance? What if there was a message to be shared? Could life be made richer by giving him a chance?

Sure enough! We got into invigorating philosophical and anthropological discussions in the shelter tonight—something I'd only been able to do with Apple. Roadblock recommended several author's names, and book titles to read.

For some reason, most of my fellow hikers hate talking about such things.

"Hey! I didn't come out here to get deep," one told me. I hadn't realized I was getting deep. I suppose depth is relative to how tall you are.

I got to thinking about Roadblock's place on this planet. Both he and I come from a long ancestry. And I mean long. Not only do we have great-great-great-great-grandparents, but also our genealogies extend back to the first generation of whatever-it-was to that point in time where and when everything began. And we did it! We got this far! The very atoms of our bodies have come a long way—far enough to acknowledge consciously the very universe that formed us. Wow! Perhaps I should save room for compassion and less room for prejudice. Our atoms precede us, and they have been around a long time. No use using them for bad vibrations. I no longer dislike Roadblock. All I had to do was remove the block in the road to move forward.

Tributaries

Delaware Water Gap. I made it.

Did Apple? Was he here? Where would I find him in this town? If I were Apple, where would I be?

"There! Apple! Hey, Apple!" I shouted, just as Apple was climbing into his brother's SUV. He backed out of the car and looked around.

"Small World! What timing," he said, clasping my hand. "This is my brother, Bob."

"Hey, Small World. I've heard a lot about you. Hop in. My wife and I would love to have you over."

I was ready for a zero day. Make that two...

Apple and I then reincorporated our joint venture and launched our enterprise together, ready for business again on the Appalachian Trail. From New Jersey, our company began to expand. First came Minstrel at Brink Road shelter.

"Watch out, the mosquitoes are horrendous," Minstrel said, waving a citronella candle around the infested shelter.

Apple and I stepped out of the cold drizzle and into the tiny shack. It would be the only times Minstrel wore a shirt: when bugs swarmed, or when it dipped below fifty degrees.

Minstrel was a talented guitarist with rock star hair.

"If I don't sing and play my guitar for more than two days, then I lose my trailname," he said, as he unwrapped his pack-Martin and tuned it. He entertained with Bob Dylan and Rolling Stones covers, as well as several clever originals.

Minstrel was a unique chef. Always last to eat, he tirelessly diced fresh garlic cloves and ginger roots, sautéing them in olive oil and eating with rice. Heads turned his way, when the aroma filled the campsite. But his breakfast concoctions were bizarre. Yeah, he had his Masters degree in chemistry from Vanderbilt, but I wasn't convinced that a bag of boiled muffin mix was a satisfying solution to breakfast.

"You just have to cook it into an edible, digestible form," he explained. "Then it's like porridge."

Oatmeal and I stuck together fine, thanks.

Next came Gizmo, a seasoned backpacker. With a 1990 AT thru-hike under his belt, he knew many Trail secrets. Gizmo was our wise man, our Gandalf of the Fellowship. He spun dazzling tales and memories of his adventures past— even about his failed thru-hike in 1974.

"I only made 600 miles," he said. "But it was then, 26 years ago, that I realized I didn't love the Rat Race as much as I loved Trail Life."

It was a simpler life for him. He was a non-materialist, if ever I saw one. Needing nothing but a backpack and a camera, Gizmo found his way from trail to trail with his photography. It was his art and livelihood.

The Company was up to four members, but Gizmo always said to think of him as an "independent contractor." He had a job to do. We'd work together often, but he wasn't on the Company's time. We respected that.

Finally, Apple, Minstrel, Gizmo, and I swept up Stormy Weather. She was a German girl with, quite possibly, the longest legs on the entire Trail. She was a jolly rancher, and when she hoofed it, she could lasso seventeen miles by lunchtime. Stormy was "big sister" and watched over the new team, making sure we enjoyed enough tea and coffee, whenever the chance arose.

"Hey, the Trail Companion book says there's a deli nearby!" she would say, gasping. She spotted every sign and note, which hinted fresh java and sandwiches. "Come on! We gotta go!"

Stormy was as much an avid a reader as she was a coffee fanatic. Her backpack was never found without a book. Never ever. Even if she had her book in her hands, there was at least one other in her pack, waiting to be read. Give her a Starbucks, a Barnes & Noble, and a zero-day, and she was lost for hours.

It was a new challenge trying to keep five hobos in business. We put a lot of stock into the Company. We had our ups and downs, but together, we would share hundreds of miles of success, deep bonds, and plenty of coffee.

Trail Tidbit #49
Names and Places

Small World meets Apple meets Minstrel meets Gizmo meets Stormy Weather, who all meet dozens of names between. Were it a connect-the-dots puzzle, names were the dots that formed a large picture; everyone on the Trail was connected through each other. Names were meaningful.

Small World. What a name, Tree said out of the blue, while I was without Company.

"I never thought it would be so significant to me," I said. "Everyone on the Trail knows me by this name—a name that's important here, but unknown off-trail."

It's unique. You are unique, said Tree. *Just like everybody else.*

"Very punny," I said. "What about you? You said to call you Tree, but there are thousands of trees here. Do I call you all Tree?"

Sure, not that it matters to us; we're all one, Tree answered.

"Well, that's just corny," I said. "Besides, that just doesn't work."

What do you mean? Tree replied. *We've been doing it for millions of years.*

I said, "If I went up to a crowd of humans and yelled, 'Hey human! Meet me at the pub in thirty minutes,' it wouldn't work. No one (or everyone) would show up. The pub might hit the jackpot if they all came, but it doesn't work for me. Even if I hollered, 'Hey Caucasian human!' it wouldn't work. We need personal names. It's not wrong to have them."

Have I argued against having personal names? Have I said anything was wrong to do? Tree asked.

"No."

What I have works for my social arrangement. We've never used names the way you do. Humans rearranged their social structure over time, and thus need names to function in their new environment. But this isn't how you've been doing it forever. We trees and plants, however, are the same now as we've been since we were first born here— long before you humans arrived. You may call me Tree, but it's for your own sake.

It's good to be called Aaron. It's good to be called Small World. It's part of your experience on Earth. But don't let that stop you from digging deeper into what you are. You are more than Aaron. Do you see that yet?

"I'm beginning to see something," I said.

You are the universe's only shot—

"… to express itself as me," I butted in. "You've said that before. I would add to it the critters and flowers and rocks and rivers and clouds and beasts. No two things are exactly alike. The universe is huge, but everything is a unique expression of it. Sacred. If only everyone knew how sacred everything is, then maybe we could save the earth."

Save the earth? Since when does the world need saved? It's been here for billions of years and has survived much greater danger than humans. And it will bounce back after you're gone, no matter what impact you have.

"Then why worry about what we do to the earth?" I asked. "Why be environmentalists and conservationists at all?"

It's for your own sake—for humans' sake. You might survive on Earth longer, not if you all become environmentalists waiting for people to rape the earth so you can protest, but rather by acting as if it's sacred to you. Mother Earth created you. You are connected to it with blood and flesh. Your body is her fruit, her vegetation, her meat. Her sacrifice. Quite literally.

"Why have we lost sight of this?" I asked.

I imagine that a big reason is because most of you focus on spiritual candy more than the sacredness of the earth. If you were focused on her, and not on the Hereafter so much, you wouldn't rape and pillage the earth.

Smack! I rubbed my head.

"You've hit on something, Tree. If there's a better place to go to when we're done here; if Earth is just a pit-stop, then 'Take what we can while we're here and get out.' God said to be fruitful and multiply; take the earth and subdue it; have dominion over everything. Well, hey! We're doing what God told us to do! Hallelujah!"

That's how it's told by those in their imaginary dominion. It's as if their God had no regard for the rest of his creation. Its only meaning was to serve Man. Not bears, not fish, not mosquitoes, not eagles, not cockroaches, not paramecium, not rats.

"I feel awful," I said. "I've lived this way my whole life. Now I've been questioning if I believe in Heaven anyway. Maybe Heaven is right here."

Heaven on Earth, Tree said

"In order to survive we must change."

It's species preservation, Small World. Every creature on Earth practices it. Only your cultural species resists change. You fear change and its implications. Go back to Galileo's day and see the truth. If the earth isn't the center of the universe, then it might imply that you're not who you thought you were. And you thought very highly of yourselves.

"We still do, apparently," I said. "And we still resist change."

You resist evolution, yes. You resist it in nature and you resist it in spirit.

"Now I'm more confused than ever," I said.

Why?

"Because I used to be so sure about everything that I believed about God, us, the world, the afterlife. Now none of it makes sense to me, yet I seem to want to hold onto it."

You see, Small World? You're resisting change. You're afraid not to believe in God. You're afraid that there may not be the afterlife you thought there to be. You're afraid.

"What kind of life is one of fear? Come to think of it, I've been afraid all my life! Afraid I'd upset God, step out of his will by making wrong choices, sinning. Afraid I'd not become what I was meant to be. Afraid I wasn't... Ugh!"

Religion has a tendency to produce such fear.

"Stupid, if you ask me," I said. "Religion."

Stupid? Believe it or not, religion is a sign of intelligence. The ability of humans to make connections between ideas and observations; their way of forming and noticing patterns in things and drawing conclusions about them—those are abilities unmatched on Earth; no other consciousness can do that.

"Except trees, of course," I said with a snicker. "Perhaps the real silly thing is keeping our conclusions in light of revelations or blatant evidence against them. That's craziness. Yet, that's what I did for so long... because I was afraid. Afraid of God's judgment for 'lack of faith.'"

If the purpose of life is to live, then you have nothing to fear. Part of living is embracing life as it is. All of it. Sacredly. Earth is your home. Live in it respectfully. Your answers are in it because your questions came from it. There are no secrets.

I felt comforted. I was beginning to feel at home, especially on the Trail. Maybe I'd never see all the answers to my questions, but I knew that I was learning to fulfill my purpose: to live. To live fully. At home. Isn't that what life is about? Here or anywhere. Life is sacred. Live and let live. Live and learn.

Top Left: The forest was alive with a mystical green ambiance at my idyllic campsite.

Right:: Aha! Delaware Water Gap! That meant that I was finally out of Pennsylvania and free from its stoney torture. Then again... does a state line mean that the rocks just vanish?

Bottom Left: Superman landed on the path again at Sunfish Pond— the southern-most body of glacial water. Apple and I had set up camp at the pristine overlook, but a riderunner spotted us and told us to leave or he'd call a ranger.

High Shock Value

If anyone knew how to complain, it was Superman. Only when he did it, you loved him for it. Superman was a Vietnam War veteran with stories that would knock you off your feet. His youthful manner in which he enjoyed things—or not—was humorous. His catch phrases were: "This is not what I had in mind," and "This wasn't in the brochure!" Aside from his talents for creative whining, Superman had a fantastic handle on metaphorical imagery.

"There's a church in Vernon that opens its doors to hikers," Gizmo told us. "For any size donation, you can use their showers, laundry machines, kitchen, and even a television."

"Oh, God! I'm there like shit on a pig!" Superman said.

By now we all were used to it. We no longer gawked at each other, thinking, *Did I just hear what I thought I heard?*

"According to the Data Book, we can hitch in on NJ 94. Let's meet there at the road crossing," Minstrel said.

Everyone's pace varied. After trudging through more New Jersey mosquito swamps, three of us waited at the road with a secured hitch.

"It's been 40 minutes," I said. "I hope Superman and Gizmo are coming."

"Gizmo said not to wait for him. He's subcontracting," said Minstrel.

Apple turned to our driver, "Thanks for waiting so long. We understand if you need to leave."

"Wait!" Minstrel said. "Is that Superman?" On the far side of the cow pasture across the road was Superman. We waved and shouted at him to hurry. Superman lifted his hiking sticks over his head and ran toward us. He looked just like an army soldier with his pack and rifle, tramping through a war zone. I wondered if he flashed back to his RTO days in the 1st Infantry Division of 1966-1968.

He landed at our feet.

"Shit," he said, gasping for air, "don't do that to me."

"We got a ride already," I said.

Superman stood upright and blurted, "Ah! That's more refreshing than a vinegar douche!"

Wide-eyed, we ducked our heads and glanced over at the driver.

"That's quite all right," he said. "I prefer Sea Breeze myself!"

We were the only ones at church that night. It was nice to find refuge away from evil New Jersey mosquitoes. Superman said, "They're like poop-flies, man! They were all over me." *Hm...*

"Superman," I said, "what brought you to the Trail?"

Superman took a seat and a handful of moments before answering. He took a deep breath and said, "I've always been close to my ex-mother-in-law. We were inspired by an article in the New Haven Register in 1968 about a guy who thru-hiked then. We planned for years to hike the AT together. Now she has cancer and not long to live. After she was diagnosed with it, she sent me the article that she had saved all these years. It was time for me to go. She lives for each step I take and my journal entries that I send home."

I looked at Superman with wonder. There was character behind his shocking personality. There was more to his story than was readily shared. The church we were in may never have witnessed such a crass man, but I doubted if it had known one so full of passion for life and loyalty to loved ones. He truly was a super man.

Trail Tidbit #51
From My Frames of Reference

Day after rainy day fogged the scenery and dotted my glasses. Hanging my specs from my collar helped little: couldn't see with them, couldn't see well without them. Didn't matter. I was looking down anyway, just so my tread-worn footwear wouldn't slip on the red New York rocks. I placed my feet flat against the open stone slabs with each step.

"Whoop!"

Thud!

"Whoa!"

Thump-de-dump-de-bumm!

"Small World, are you OK?" Apple called, after I landed several yards down the slope.

It wasn't the first fall of the day (nor would it be the last), but at least I wasn't hurt. Apple took my arm to help me up.

"Damn, you're heavy. Where's Minstrel when you need him?" he said with a grunt.

"Bite me, beanpole," I said, laughing. "I don't need your help."

Miles later, I screeched to a halt.

"Apple," I said. He didn't hear me. "Apple!"

"Yeah?" he called, still hiking.

"Wait!"

"Why? What's wrong?" he asked, turning around.

"My glasses. I lost my glasses. They're gone! I had them hanging on my collar."

Apple whistled an *Oh, crap!*

"I must have lost them when I fell."

"You wanna go back and get them?" Apple asked.

"It's too late in the day," I reasoned. "That was several miles ago and there's no guarantee that I'd find them. Besides, not only would I have to hike there, but I'd also have to hike the miles back. I'd never make it to the shelter before dark."

"I'll go with you," Apple assured.

"No. Maybe someone will find them. I'll leave a note in the shelter. That prescription was four years old, anyway."

"Superman said that his eyes have improved throughout the Trail. Maybe yours will, too," Apple said.

Jumping forward two months to my home in the Midwest, I would receive a package in the mail from friends Hokey Pokey and Mad Dog. The box contained my glasses and a letter written on the reverse side of a Burger King place-mat:

Dear Small World,

So there we were hiking along the first of October on a fine sunny day. Neither Mad Dog nor I can resist a shelter register so we popped in at Wildcat Shelter, N.Y. for a short break and read. Mad Dog sniffed around the shelter checking on all the leavings—pots, candles, books and glasses. *He put the glasses on and thought he looked very clever (I thought goofy). He said that the glasses looked like yours. At that same time I found your register entry and plea for the return of your glasses. Hallelujah! What a coincidence!*

The coincidence was even more astounding than they knew: Hokey Pokey and Mad Dog had found my specs on the very last day I was on the Trail!

But that was months away, and I was getting headaches daily and had trouble focusing. I had to find a town with an eye doctor to get new glasses. The Trail Companion book said there was one in Great Barrington, Massachusetts. I'd squint and pucker my eyes all the way there.

Trail Tidbit #52
No Room at the Inn

Journal Entry
8/10/00—From Glen Brook Lean-to to Great Barrington, MA (7.9 miles)

As we crossed US 7, Stormy Weather thundered, "Look! A farmer's market! Peaches!"

We hunched around a flimsy plastic table, sinking our teeth into fresh nectarines, peaches, and grapes. Juice ran down my arms to my elbow. It dripped off my beard.

Great Barrington was a few miles down the road.

"I gotta go into town to get my eyes examined and order some glasses," I said. I've lost faith that my eyes will heal or that my old frames would appear.

"We might as well come, too," said Minstrel. "We'll stick together."

"There might be a coffee shop," said Stormy, "or a bookstore!"

We hitched a ride in a van littered with cornhusks. Minstrel watched over our clothes at the laundromat. Stormy went shopping. Apple went with me to Berkshire Eye Center to give a second opinion on new frames. They cost me a small fortune, but at least I won't have headaches all the time. My new spectacles will be sent to Cheshire, MA when they're finished. General Delivery. I'll pick them up from the post office when I get there.

It was too late in the day to get back to the Trail and find a place to camp before dark. There was a music festival in town, and only one motel had vacancy. Minstrel had called the 1-800 number to the Comfort Inn and was told that reservations were unnecessary—if we went "now," since we needed to pay cash.

Perfect.

All four of us piled into a truck and rode to the Inn.

"I'm sorry," said the clerk behind the counter, "we have no rooms, except for a king-size, which I cannot fill with four people."

Crap! Our options were out. What to do?

"But we'd just heard they had rooms," said Stormy.

"I think we're being given the 'run-around' because we're stinky hikers, and they can make more money from those attending the festival," I said.

"Wait here," Minstrel said. "I've got to make a phone call."

Minstrel spotted a pay-phone outside.

1-800—

Ingenious.

The National Comfort Inn phone service's computers revealed vacancy—for a room, without the jacked-up-music-festival-price. Minstrel secured a room with his bankcard and marched up to the Inn's front desk.

"Hi," he said, like he'd never been there before. "I have a reservation for Easterly."

The clerk was floored. He fidgeted and fumbled around, not knowing what to do.

How devilish, I thought. *We caught him red-handed.*

The clerk called his manager.

We got the king-size room for the regular rate and crashed there with a pizza.

"Guess what guys," I said, holding open my Data Book. "From here to Katahdin, it figures to be exactly 666.6 miles."

Trail Tidbit #53
"Berried" Treasures

Serendipitous moments popped up in many forms on the Trail, but few matched the capture of rapture experienced, when stumbling upon treasure troves of tart and tasty treats: berries. A fulfilling fortuitous find, these glorious gatherings were gratefully gained by an always-hungry hiker.

Plenty of prosperous pickings presented themselves as early as the Blue Ridge Mountains. Blueberry bunches beckoned me beside the byway day after day, mile after mile. So I partook of the palate-pleasing products of Nature. Oh, what punch of flavor to savor, wild berries are! Commercial crops comparatively pale to those I found along the Trail; strawberries, blackberries, blueberries, brambleberries, and raspberries. Pluck to perk up plain old porridge, or simply sample a bowl of berries-and-cream, trail-style; powdered milk, sugar, fresh berries. Just add water.

Eating berries two-fisted was a delight I'd not had in civilization. Store-bought berries were pricey, thus rarely found in my refrigerator. Recollecting mother's summer fruit salads, I remembered how every berry was cherished, eaten in slow motion. In the mountains, however, the price is right. I gobbled handfuls of plump, juicy berries as often as I could. Fantastic! It's not gluttony; it's grateful gastronomic glee.

"Today we pass by a blueberry farm," Apple said. Minstrel, Stormy, Apple, and I approached in anticipation of ample apportions, eyeing boundless beds of beautiful bushes bespeckled with the biggest blueberries I'd ever beheld.

Tasting one, I was armed with a bucket, ready to plunder a harvest. But then our hopes were dashed, as we sensed something surly soon to precipitate: rain. And it was cold! Not having the appropriate attire, I acknowledged I ought to abandon ship and amble onward to keep warm.

Following a few miles, the pour-down pulled out, pacifying paces, and the puddle-painted pathway pulled up to the grandest blueberry bush I'd never before beheld—ten feet high. And it was a cultivation of Creation; Mother Nature's nourishment—the kind I preferred—free for the taking.

Mother Nature seemed to conspire to enlighten anyone, whose desire was to enjoy her and know her. Moments such as these were part of what the Trail was about. I was thankful for such gifts. The Community of Life in the Outdoors may be a Small World, but it truly is the Real World. All else is manmade.

Trail Tidbit #54
Weather or Not, Here I Come!

Whether weather's warm or wintry, what one wants is wonder. I craved adventure. I was a discoverer, an explorer. I was Henry David Thoreau, Meriwether Lewis, Bilbo Baggins. Take me over craggy mountaintops. Lead me through dark woods and swampy valleys. Throw wind in my face. Snow. Sleet. Anything but rain! Please, no rain. The timbre of my soul couldn't bear the mood swings of the weather's ax.

Imagine a perfect day to hike: first waking in your sun-warmed tent to the sounds of birds greeting the day and a chipper creek at play. It's the kind of day, which begins with a good stretch and yawn, as if to suck in the green life surrounding you. The forest had so much to say, lots to teach. And Tree followed me, wherever I went.

Enjoy the moss-covered boulders and logs, Tree said. *Taste the cool morning air. Feel the dual texture of sunlight and breeze on your skin. Let the Outside come in.*

"Ah, so peaceful, hopeful. I feel so vibrant and alive!" I said.

Life begets life, Tree breathed. *Turn your Inside out. Energy creates energy. Complete the circle.*

I took a deep breath.

In through the nose, out through the mouth.

I breathed in forest and exhaled thankfulness. I touched the soft mosses, smelled the wild flowers, and watched scurrying animals, listening to their sounds.

"Ah, life is good," I sighed.

Tree agreed, adding, *And to think that all of this occurs and exists despite the world you've created "out there." Always has.*

My boots choked and sputtered to a stop. Up or down the Trail no one was coming, so I stepped off the pathway and walked twenty yards into the trees and sat on a boulder. I had had an appointment with Tree. He showed up wearing a chunky bark jacket with long green needle-like fringes. I thought I must have been the only person in the world who knew this tree existed, who ever gazed upon its splendor.

Life is not only what you experience as you build your empires and tend to your chores and ponder your careers, Tree said. *Yet your people often act as if you're all there is, as if you are the sum of Creation.*

"That's true," I said. "But we destroy nearly everything in our path, including ourselves."

Perhaps when you're all gone, we can finally survive.

"In harmony..."

Harmony? Doesn't everything live in harmony?

"Of course not!" I said.

Sure it does.

"So, if I were to bulldoze this entire forest, you'd call that living harmoniously?"

What would happen if you were to plow this forest down?

"Nearly everything would be wiped out."

Exactly.

"And you call that harmony?"

Harmony complements melody. Think of it this way: Aaron climbs to the top of a fifty-story building and tosses a brick over the edge. The brick plummets to the earth and squishes a grasshopper on the sidewalk below. That would be harmonious.

"How so?" I asked.

What is the melody in my little story?

"Aaron climbs building with brick. Throws brick. Brick lands."

Very good. Now harmony is the consequence of melody. Had the brick floated in the air, then that would have been disharmonious. Had the brick landed flat on the grasshopper, and the grasshopper lived on to tell its grandbugs about it, then that would have been disharmonious. If you plowed down this forest and the trees survived, then that would have been disharmonious. Each consequence follows the melody smoothly, making harmony.

"I understand. Man is not the melody."

Right. You're beautiful notes on the page, but not the only notes. And even melody harmonizes with harmony.

"So if Man rapes and pillages the Earth, leaving nothing for himself in years to come, he would die off. It would only be expected."

That would be harmony.

"But if we rape and pillage the Earth, and she continued to support us, as we continue to live that lifestyle, then that would be disharmonious."

You're catching on.

"Geez. I need to change my tune. But how?" I asked.

K-k-ka-ka-boom!

Lightning. Thunder. Rain.

I bolted up from my rock, threw on my Gortex jacket and backpack and left Tree without a good-bye.

Rain.

Rivers from the sky plunged down for hours. I was glad I had stuffed my clothes in a plastic garbage bag to keep dry inside my pack.

Rain.

The Trail became a streambed of gushing water. I stayed to the sides of the Trail, hoping to keep my feet dry.

Rain.

It bounced off my Gortex jacket, but I was soaked to the bone with sweat anyway. So much for Gortex.

Rain.

"No! Dammit! Stop!"

Slosh, slosh, slosh.

Water gurgled between my toes with each step.

"Oh, it's hopeless!" I huffed. And like a stomping crybaby, I trampled through the flooded pathway, kicking water everywhere.

When the rain let up hours later, I made camp and crawled into my tent. Each sock wrung out like a dishrag, and my shorts slid off with a *slop*.

It'll pass by morning, I hoped.

Rain. Rain.

That night, my tent gave up the ghost and began to leak... again. Right on my face.

Tik. Tik. Tik. Tik.

I was like a stubborn showoff, playing *Chicken* to see who'd crack first.

Tik. Tik. Tik. Tik.

I was *not* going to let it win, dammit! It was dark, chilly, and lonely in the tent.

Tik. Tik. Tik.

Where was Apple and the Company?

Tik. Tik.

"They must be at a shelter."

Tik.

"That's a melody I'd whistle to..."

Rain.

Rain, but no *tik, tik, tik.*

The slow leak had followed a line down the side of the tent and streamed away from my face. I won.

Harmony. I fell asleep. Morning came without the rain. What would the new day bring? First, it gave me two wet socks and boots to slide into. Next, I wriggled into my cold, soggy shirt and shorts. "I smell like a sheep," I said, grabbing my sopping toilet paper.

Wind had shaken most of the water off my tent, but it was beginning to sprinkle. A wet tent was a heavy tent, so I bundled everything up and wrapped my rain cover around it, before the drizzle metamorphosed into another downpour.

Golf ball size raindrops bounced off everything. I groaned at the sky. My spirits were dampened. Sputtering and muttering, I had zipped up, packed up, and tied up, but I was unable to buck up. Sarcasm precipitated likewise.

"Yeehaw... what a view. I can see ten feet in any direction!"

I cursed Mother Nature, whom I had blessed the day before. Bitterness, frustration, and resentment kicked aside my delight and thrill of the Trail.

What's wrong with you? This is the Trail. Shouldn't there be beauty in such a day?

"Huh?" I said. "On a day like this?"

Isn't there loveliness in the rolling clouds in front of you, the glistening leaves around you, the spongy ground beneath you, the pitter-patter of water droplets upon you?

"I hate hiking in bad weather!" I yelled.

Can't you see? There's no such thing as "bad" weather. If you will not learn to appreciate Mother Nature's every face, then you choose misery.

Just then, a small patch of blue sky winked at me. My spirits soared. But my hopes were dashed, as it closed in with clouds. Then a ray of light hit me in the face. I was afraid to look up. What were my chances of lasting sunshine? I rolled my eyes up from under my brow to peek at the sky. A vast blue giant was unraveling the cotton dress above. I choked up.

You're becoming thankful for the little things in life, said Tree.

"It's the sadness that makes the happiness so happy!" I reminded myself. "If it were not for the rain, would I love the open skies as much?"

If it were not for the rain, none of us would live to.

I had thought the Great Smokies (a.k.a. Great Soakies) were rough, but they were parched compared to New England. Three out of four days bore rain or overcast skies from Pennsylvania to Vermont. Small lakes formed on mountaintops. A gentleman in Cheshire, Massachusetts declared, "This is the most rain we've had in one season for 70 years. They said there was only a 20% chance of rain yesterday. It rained all day. Today, they called an 80% chance of rain, and it's dry. Well, I'm on my way to the casinos then. With odds like that, I'll take it as a sign to hit the slot machines!"

Crying Wolf used to say, "You will not conquer the mountains. Hell, they've been here for millions of years. Learn from them and follow their lead to live among them. Then you will succeed to your destination."

The Trail is what it is and will not change. It's not bad or good. It just is.

It was futile getting angry about the rain, fog, or another steep ascent. That's the Trail. *Don't try to conquer it or it will conquer you.*

As I went with the Trail's flow, I would learn to anticipate and appreciate whatever would precipitate—to hear the melody and sing along.

Left: A New York Apple scaled the slick boulder with ease.

Top Right: I stuck out my thumb with Apple, Gizmo, Stormy Weather and Minstrel (who snapped our photo). Drivers honked, laughed and shouted at us from their car windows.

Bottom Right: Minstrel, Apple, Stormy Weather and I became a well-oiled train on the AT. Gizmo was a detached caboose, but a welcome addition anytime. We bathed here along the Housatonic River.

Trail Tidbit #55
Wondering

Whether weather's warm or wintry,
What one wants is wonder;
Delicious days, dawn to dusk,
Delightfully to don their

Light and Life, loudly lauding
Love to all who will lend ear.

Saying,
"Know I naught, but these three things;
One Law that I am under:
Hope, Love, and Faith in what's Real,
Which will not tear asunder
Your body, mind, and soul—I serve,
Never rape nor plunder.

Rather,
Peace I give to you like trees,
And joy as loud as thunder;
Because,
"Whether weather's warm or wintry
What we want is wonder!"

Top Left: Stormy Weather, Apple, and Minstrel lifted this boulder out of the trailway—those things could be such a nuisance, you know.

Top Right: Rainy day after day made muddy trails that caked to my boots, making them heavy.

Bottom: At Upper Good Pond cabin, Apple captured attention with stories. Minstrel played a medley on his Martin pack-guitar, and I sang my jazzy "Wondering" song with him.

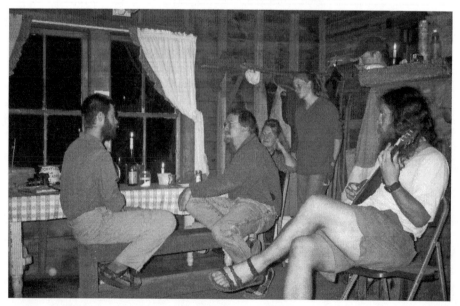

Trail Tidbit #56
R.I.P.

News traveled quickly on the Trail through shelter registers, words of mouth, or mail pickups.

"Did you hear that Latestart is off the Trail?"

"Did you hear that Red Eye's fuel container exploded?"

"Did you hear about the hiker, who tore a ligament in her knee?"

"Did you hear that Mrs. Recycled Teenager had to be helicoptered off the Trail with several broken bones?"

"Did you hear that Lady Kat got bursitis?"

Bursitis in the hips had swayed Lady Kat's resignation from the Trail in Connecticut. So close to Katahdin, oh so close... Everyone was sorry to hear this news; we shared her passion for the Trail and desire to reach Maine. But "time wounds all heels," knees, or hips: a Trail-truth we all had to face sooner or later. I'm still convinced, however, that Lady Kat will climb Katahdin someday after she mends. "Time heals all wounds."

The last quarter of the Trail was thinning out; hikers were peeling away. Then news came, which shocked my spirits. And the Trail fell silent for many days.

"Crash '60 is dead."

"Crash 1960 was found sitting on a rocky mountain overlook with a snack in his hand. He'd had a heart attack. He was only forty years old."

I didn't know Crash '60 well, but the image burned in my mind.

One last terrestrial pleasure before slipping into the celestial....

It gave me chills to think about, the good kind, although cheerless.

Did he know he was leaving? Is that why he came to the Trail?

My heart throbbed a few extra beats for his family. May they carry on with peace and well-being.

Happy trails, Crash.

Trail Tidbit #57
I Scream, Ice Cream!

Two things disappeared, when we crossed the border into Vermont: the rain, and Apple's last pound of fat.

"Apple, you look emaciated," I said.

"I feel weak," he replied. "All the time. I'm so tired."

"Maybe you should see a doctor," said Minstrel.

"Great idea!" said Stormy. "Then while we're in town, we can stop for coffee, or something."

The doctor diagnosed Apple as slightly anemic and prescribed a change in diet, high in iron and fat-rich foods: peanut butter, cheeses, breads....

"Let's give Apple a jump-start," I said. "How about ice cream?"

"We need to celebrate, anyway," Stormy said. "Vermont!"

"Not only Vermont," Apple said. "I have to fax the signed forms for a new home. My wife and I will be moving together to a new home in the D.C. suburbs. She's going to school there."

"Fantastic!" I said. "That's worth celebrating!"

"Ben & Jerry's!" Stormy squeaked.

Vermont was the home of Ben & Jerry's ice cream. Where else could Vermont be better celebrated than at a Ben & Jerry's scoopshop? We stormed the heavenly gates of one in Manchester Center. We were on a mission.

"Welcome!" announced the chap behind the counter, "What can I get ya?"

Oh, we knew exactly what we wanted… the *Vermonster.* Twenty scoops of ice cream, three chocolate brownies, four bananas, whipped cream, hot-fudge, sprinkles, and four spoons, please!

"Ah, of course!" nodded the happy attendant. "Choose your flavors."

Stormy, Minstrel, Apple, and I chose five different flavors each. Like giddy children before a lit birthday cake, we watched the scoop-steward dig into each barrel of frozen delicacy. Finally, with grandeur, he upheld his masterpiece like a proud painter.

"Ohh! Ahh!"

"Poor Gizmo—out subcontracting. We'll have to eat this all by ourselves," Stormy said.

An audience stared at us, as if we'd just walked on stage pant-less.

"Time us!" we said to the ice-cream clerk.

We held up our spoons. "To Vermont! To Apple!"

Every bite was a chilling experience, filling our mouths with ecstasy and delight. Taste buds burst with elation upon every spoonful. Spoons clinked together, as if sword fighting. No one said anything but "Oh! Mmm! Try this!" Eight minutes later, the entire mound had vanished. The *Vermonster* had been slain. We gave ourselves a standing ovation and marched directly to the local breakfast hotspot for pancakes, eggs and sausage. We *had* to celebrate. Besides, Apple needed some fattening up.

Trail Tidbit #58
Attitude Adjustments

Garbage in, garbage out," I said over a spoonful of instant mashed potatoes. "I noticed something today. When I'm in a bad mood or think negative thoughts, my hiking goes downhill (no pun intended)."

Apple replied, "I hear ya. It's like milking a cow."

"What?"

"Like milking a cow. Each time you squeeze an utter, the decrease in milk increases the cow's internal void of milk."

"Geez, Apple. You've spent too much time on the farm. But it's true. I have a decrease in milk when I increase the negative space inside. Yikes... the Tao of Cow."

"Its goofy, but it works," Apple said.

"Sounds heady, for a cow."

"Unless you're bullheaded..."

I put it to the test. When downbeat, angry thoughts arose, I learned to say to myself, "Save your energy for the Trail." And if I swapped out the negative tones with upbeat ones, my rhythm increased. My breathing improved. My legs chugged like an engine. The Tao of Cow.

Out with the old, in with the new.

"There was a time when I *lived* for the scenic views," I said over a Vermont vista.

Apple replied, "Yeah. I used to get depressed, when there was nothing but trees to see."

"Me too. But now I don't even notice when there are no overlooks, or lakes, or whatever. I notice when there *are*, but I live for the hike itself now."

Walking was my vocation, and the wilderness was my home. I felt at ease with the routine and environment.

"You know, this all just seems so natural now, doesn't it?" I said. "I mean, it's like learning a language. When I lived in Germany, I struggled with the language for months. I came home, feeling like I learned very little. But upon my next visit, I couldn't believe how much I was able to understand and speak. That's how I feel now: as if I've returned."

I now hiked for hike's sake and loved it. My attitudes had changed. I was at home in the woods.

That was then, this is now.

"It took me months to stop treating miles like an enemy," I said over ten miles into the day.

Apple replied, "No kidding. I used to count them daily for some assumed deadline."

Now they were a game. We tried to reach our target, like the weatherman, who compared his forecast with the actual degrees to see how close he came. We still wanted to climb Katahdin on October 1 (my birthday), but we didn't fret about it. Instead, we gobbled up the adventure that each day offered.

"Do you realize that we have only 500 miles left to go?" I asked.

Apple whistled an *Unbelievable!*

"Man, do you remember the first 500 miles?"

"I sure do," Apple said. "I was so impressed with myself. 'Holy cow, 500 miles! That's so much!'"

"Yeah. Now we have only 500 miles left, and it seems like nothing."

Attitude was everything.

Trail Tidbit #59
Stars and Stripes

Look for the big red barn when you cross VT 12," said the southbounder. "You can't miss it."

"And you say we can stay there?" I asked.

"In exchange for work, yes. Dan, the homeowner, put a showerhead under the deck, which you can use, too."

"Great! After twenty miles, a shower will be worth some weeding in the garden."

After chores that evening, Sunny Campfire, Pat From Maine, Nomad, and the Company (including our subcontractor, Gizmo) gathered around the picnic table in the dark to cook dinner. I looked up at the sky and asked, "What's that whitish haze streaked across the sky?"

Pat From Maine said, "That's the Milky Way, Small World."

"No way!" I couldn't believe it. "I've never seen the Milky Way before!"

"You're kidding," Nomad said.

Where I grew up, light pollution hung like a veil over the sky, hiding her sparkling face. My dream had always been to behold the vast heavens chockfull of stars. There it was.

"Why haven't I noticed it before on the Trail?"

"Too many trees?" said Sunny Campfire.

We watched the sky show off its meteorites, satellites, the Milky Way, and millions of stars. The bright Chicago skyline couldn't hold a candle to the Universe. I was spellbound. How far away was that satellite? That planet? That star? What a small world we were. In a galaxy... far, far away, I was enthralled. Mesmerized. Alive.

Earth's closest star climbed over the horizon and peeked at me in my tent. It was time to get up and work. Dan had offered us a deal.

"In exchange for a couple hours of work," he had said, "I will drive you north to Hanover, New Hampshire. You can slack-pack back to my place. Then, give me some time the next morning, and I will drive you back to Hanover, and you can continue from there."

Sounded like a plan. So, I was southbound for a day.

New faces arrived at Dan's place. Yellow-blazers. Meet *les Misérables:* the wretched ones, who followed the yellow stripes on the road, rather than the white ones on the Trail. Most Defenders of the Thru-hiker Title despised yellow-blazers. I mean, how could you call yourself a Thru-hiker, when you weren't hiking all the way *through?* Passions arose.

One purist bellowed, "I stay away from Yellow-blazers. I don't want anyone to think I'm one of them."

"I earned my stripes," said another, "and I'm not talking about yellow ones!"

Others barked, "I won't even climb Katahdin with a Yellow-blazer. What, share the glory? Heck, maybe they won't even summit... since you can't *drive* up!"

The problem wasn't the fact that they were Yellow-blazers, but that they tried to hide it, telling everyone that they actually hiked 2,000 miles. The nerve. Everyone knew who they were; they were easy to spot. Yellow-blazers often wore the mark of civilization—a particular fabric; a desecration to the earned title *Thru-hiker.* Cotton! Cotton kills. Cotton doesn't work on the Trail. Everyone knew that. It holds moisture and dries slowly. It's abrasive. It's weak. It's heavy. It's not good.

Uh-oh. I can hear it now: "Hike your own hike." Right?

But blue jeans? Never. Now that was a sacrilege!

Another notable trait of Yellow-blazers was that they were always ahead of us. After morning chores, Dan dropped us off in Hanover, as promised. And who should be there already, but the Yellow-blazers?

"How did you guys get here so fast? That's over 20 miles," I said.

"Oh, we're fast, I guess."

I guess? Pretty bad guess if you asked me.

Who were they trying to fool?

Why did they want the label *Thru-hiker* if their ingredients didn't match?

Laugh it off, I thought. *Let them live with themselves, if they can.*

I may have been an occasional slack-packer, or even a southbounder, but I was determined to be nothing less than a Thru-hiker. Two States left.

Top Left: It was in Vermont that I finally noticed how powerful my trail legs and lungs had become. I was able to climb rugged terrain and still breathe through my nose, filling my chest with treasures of balsam fir fragrances.

Right: Atop Stratton Mountain, next to the firetower, was where the mount's caretaker (Hugh) lived half the year. It's also where the Long Trail splits from the AT... I'd been hiking two trails at the same time!

Bottom Left: I sat among flitting hummingbirds at William B. Douglas shelter, cooking my supper.

Trail Tidbit #60
Legacy Under Fire

I f I were a great ship with torn sails, I would rather sink. For what is a sailboat without its sails? It's like a ghost—sad, drifting—looking for home.

The AT is like a great ship with good sails. See her glory? She goes places; sees people. She makes dreams come true. Her decks tell tales of legends and heroes, whom she carried to far away lands. Each generation is a part of her legacy. They inherit the wind in her sails, the breath of her life.

Wait!
What are you doing?
Why are you *tearing* her sails?
Please. Stop!
Why?!
W—what's the ax for?
No. No! Please!
Not the mast! I beg of you.
Not the mast....

Has the Great Ship lost its sails? A pilgrimage made easy isn't worth the quest. Don't people see that on the Trail? Don't people respect that off the Trail? Do we love the Trail? Of course we do. Do we love the Trail to death?

Sometimes I feared that the Trail's honor and glory would soon fade like a ghost ship. Lost at sea. No sails. No mast. Just drifting. No legacy.

An undercurrent along the Trail was, "I am the Captain of this ship. And I need no crew!" A spoiled generation of pilgrims seemed to feel that it was no longer its "crewmate's keeper." I saw how they cruised along without regard for others on or off the AT.

The numbers of hikers thinned the farther north I went. The Company had found itself in a bubble: days of land separating us from the hikers ahead and those behind. But we followed a messy trail of inconsiderate, obnoxious bottom-feeders for hundreds of miles. They plowed through the Trail like a bulldozer, digging graves for everyone behind them.

"I'm sorry," said a hostel caretaker, "no more hikers. We've had enough of their abuse."

"After this year, it's over," said the janitor of a church. "We had to hire a work crew yesterday to clean up the mess made by the group of hikers before you. Here's a list of hikers who were here." He handed us the register.

"Yup. Many of the same people we've had trouble with in the past," we said.

"Please say something to them, when you see them next," said the janitor.

And we did. But they were flippant and brushed us off.

A fraternity at Dartmouth College opened its basement to AT hikers. Sleepers were piled in one room, party animals in the other. But no one could sleep. The racket and marijuana smoke was too heavy. I asked the crazy bunch to settle down. So did Gizmo. But they couldn't have cared less. Gizmo went to sleep outside.

After the weed burned up, and the harmonica lost its life, I started to dream. Finally. In dreamland, I saw a stream. *Trickle, trickle* it flowed.

Hold it!

Whoa!

That's not trickle, trickle!

That's tinkle, tinkle!

It can't be—better not be—what I think it is...

It was.

I scrounged for my flashlight to shed some light on the matter. What was the matter? The matter was puddling on the floor, as a forty-year-old kid pissed next to Gizmo's equipment.

"Are you drunk?!" I shouted.

He didn't respond. He *was* smashed.

In the morning, before his conscious mind pretended to be awake, I placed a bucket of hot soapy water next to his mattress with a note, asking him to clean up his mess and to stop behaving so childishly—giving hikers a bad reputation. He got livid.

"It was an accident," he said. "I thought I was in my tent!"

"We believe you," I said, "but that's not the point."

Gizmo tiptoed around the pee puddle to pick up his backpack.

"I can't help it if I was drunk!"

"When you're invited into somebody else's home, you don't *get* drunk," Gizmo said. "Especially if you know you've had a bad history of drunken behavior."

Mr. Pisser geared himself up to strike a blow. Apple and I stepped in. He was sober enough to know that if he threw a punch at Gizmo, then he'd have the whole punchbowl to deal with. We would have given him one hell of a hangover.

Why is this apathy seeping into the Trail? Isn't the Trail life a subculture with a different vision than what we left behind? Why take the restlessness and hubbub with you on the Trail? It's not a dog-eat-dog Trail. It's not a prison, where each must fend for himself and demand his "rights." Isn't hiking the AT a pilgrimage for you, too? A vision quest? Think. Feel. Feel free.

I would like to believe that everyone's hopes and plans were pure in the beginning. But when the outside world exploited the Trail, I think it broke people. Don't get me wrong. Towns and Angels were an extraordinary part of the Trail experience. But the entire Trail could be done through a credit card today. And so many people wanted to make a buck off a hiker.

Want a shower? Two bucks.

Want a ride? Five dollars.

Want a room? We made a new Bed & Breakfast specifically designed for hikers like you! Thirty pieces of silver, please!

Maybe that's what has got into these poor hikers: their dreams were smashed by the very disillusions and exploitation they were running from. Their great ship began to rock in the storm. I can still hear their frantic screams, as the wind whipped around the boat.

"The sails! The sails!"

The Appalachian Trail is still a great ship, and its crew is still strong. May we learn from the legends and heroes, however, who sailed before us. May future hikers be mindful of these things before it's too late.

Trail Tidbit #61
Weakened: Freeday, Scatterday, Sundry

The sun gave the morning a warm hug. The muggy air gave me a sloppy kiss. I wiped it off and sat up in my tent.

"I can't do it."

I'm tired.

I can't do nineteen miles today.

I don't feel well.

I don't want to go that far.

I'm tired.

I crawled out of my tent and lowered my food bag from the tree to grab a Pop-Tart. Apple was already eating his breakfast.

"Apple?" I said. "Can we talk?"

"Of course," he answered. "Are you okay? You don't look good."

I put down my Pop-Tart. "I'm tired, Apple. I can't do this."

"Can't do what?"

"The group thing. I'm so sorry. I like Minstrel and Stormy and Gizmo, but it's too much."

"What do you mean?" Apple asked. He scooped up another spoonful of oatmeal.

"I feel like I'm hiking someone else's hike," I said. "Go when the group goes. Stop when it stops. Wait when the group's not ready to go. Go when I'm not ready to go."

"I noticed you've been breaking away a bit," Apple said.

"Yeah. I just didn't want to say anything. I don't want to let anyone down. It seems we've all put a lot of stock into this group."

"Right. We all thought we'd climb Katahdin together."

"Now I understand why Gizmo is a 'subcontractor,'" I said. "I just want to be me."

"That's one thing I've noticed about you, Small World. You've always been true to yourself."

"Thanks, Apple. Your friendship means a lot to me. I wish things could be the way they were. And I understand if you want to stick with the group."

Twelve miles later, I stopped at a shelter for rest. Minstrel and Stormy had flown ahead of me, headed for the next shelter, another seven miles farther. Apple wasn't far behind me. I opened the shelter register to see if Minstrel and Stormy had left a note for us.

"It's a hot one!" Apple said, when he arrived, smudging his brow.

"Look here," I said. "Minstrel wrote in the register, 'It looks like our group has disbanded. Stormy and I have moved on.'"

"Just like that..." Apple said.

" I guess they noticed that I was distancing myself," I said.

Apple sighed. "I think we've all had similar feelings. You're just the first to act on it."

I put down the register notebook. "I'm staying here tonight. I can't make another seven miles."

Apple unbuckled his backpack. "I'll stay with you."

The summit of Mt. Moosilauke was both a joy and a disappointment: we were happy to reach the first mountain above treeline, but an ominous cloud had veiled it. And it was cold! Sunny Campfire, Pat From Maine, Apple and I took a break at treeline. Pat said, "I'm meeting my son in town..." Everyone thought she said, "I'm eating my son..." Pat's new trailname became Cannibal Pat.

Posing at Mt. Moosilauke's summit was Apple, Small World (me), Cannibal Pat, Gizmo, Sunny Campfire, Tex, and Pipeline.

Gizmo, a professional photographer, did what came natural to him, as Apple and I posed.

Fruitful Living

My brain had hashed through everything I could think of a thousand times. What more could I think about as I kept rhythm on the Trail? I needed some food for thought.

Tree was often the one with fresh meat: *Why was it Gizmo said he was a vegetarian?*

"Well," I said, "he just doesn't see meat as food."

Tell me about what you ate today.

"The same old breakfast. For lunch I had some Vermont cheese, a bagel, a Powerbar, some Trailmix, jerky, and a vitamin."

Tree swayed back. *It's a miracle you're still alive. Talk about unreal food!*

"Why do you say that?" I asked.

Your diet is dead and processed, Tree answered.

"It seems to be working so far," I said. "In fact, almost all Americans eat this way."

Yet you're the sickest species on Earth.

"True, true," I said. "And the fattest. We just don't get enough exercise."

That may be so, said Tree, *but exercise takes second chair to food.*

"At least I'm taking my vitamins," I said.

That vitamin is dead, said Tree. P*lant it in the ground like a seed. Nothing will sprout. It only affects your body in a symptomatic way. It's not deep cellular nutrition. It's not real food at all. Nothing in your backpack is.*

"I have some dehydrated veggies in there. There's dried fruit in my trailmix. Most of it I dehydrated myself at home," I said.

All dead.

"Dead? How so?"

Heat from the dehydrating process, Tree explained. *The life force begins to die at 105° F.*

I held up a hand. "That's why high fevers can be so dangerous," I said.

Right. And boiling point is twice that. Humans are the only species on the planet that cooks its food. Everyone else eats only raw foods. And they're healthier for it. Life begets life. Death and dead foods beget death and disease.

"At least we have medicine," I said.

Doctors are dying from the same diseases and at the same pace as everyone else because their diets are the same.

"Yikes," I said. "A lot of good our drugs do."

Not much at all... besides, the side effects are horrendous, often cancerous.

"But on the Trail, I cannot carry raw foods. Fresh fruits and vegetables are too expensive and heavy to carry on my back."

I understand. And you can't forage your day away. That's why I didn't bring up the issue until now. But you can choose life after the Trail.

"I'd like to. It seems to be the right thing to do," I said.

It's not an issue of right or wrong. As with most things, it's an issue of what's best for you, said Tree.

"What about meat?" I asked. "We have to cook that."

Again, there's no moral issue here, but I'd suggest you look at some interesting points. It appears that your body is adapted to particular types of food. For example, your teeth. Wolves have flesh-tearing teeth. You don't.

"That's why we cook our meat," I argued.

Fine. But the wolf also has an extremely high hydrochloric acid content in its stomach to break down meat. Humans have a much smaller amount. And consider the wolf's digestive tract. Very short. Humans have very long tracts. The meat sits there for too long and putrefies, ferments, and releases toxins.

"I see. No wonder I get indigestion when I eat too much meat."

Some people feel better after eating meat. There's no single right way. I'm just giving you some food for thought.

"We need protein, don't we?"

Yes, but not as much as the Meat and Dairy Council tell you that you do.

They also like to tell you how important calcium is to your body, and where to get it.

"Cows," I said. "Milk."

Where do the cows get their protein and calcium? Tree asked. *Easy. From the grains and vegetation they graze. Have you ever thought about why humans are the only species that drink another animal's milk? Most humans drink it their whole lives. Even the calf is kicked away after a year. Mama cow says, "Learn to graze, kid!"*

"I just thought of something else," I said. "Even the milk we drink is dead. It's been pasteurized and homogenized."

Not to mention filled with hormones and steroids, Tree added. *In such a state, the calcium and protein cannot be properly absorbed and put to use in the body.*

"Geez," I said. "What are we doing? Why do we do this?"

Convenience. Ignorance. Exploitation. Carelessness. Habit. You choose the reason. But you can choose what you will do from now on.

I shook my head. "I want real food!"

Trail Tidbit #63
Appalachian Money Club

The AT was a long thread, stitching together a fabulous earthen quilt. Threading the AT through the eye of the needle—the White Mountains—was tough. Among the most ruggedly beautiful, the White Mountains were also the least welcoming.

The Thread often strung itself above treeline through the Whites. Camping above treeline, however, was neither permitted nor wise. And the forests were so dense, and the ground was so craggy that tent space was scant. We were forced to use areas woven by the Appalachian Mountain Club (AMC): shelters, tent platforms, or huts. And nothing was available on AMC trails without fee.

Sleep in our shelter: just *ten dollars.*

Pitch your tent on our platform for only *six bucks.*

Stay in the hut? Sixty fat ones!

My budget was tight after sewing nearly 1,800 miles together. I had wanted to take my time through the Whites. To let myself unspool in their splendor. Impossible. Too expensive. Instead, I hiked as fast and far as I could each day, just to save money. At the end of each day, I still had to camp. There was nothing more annoying than having no place to go and being charged to use a shelter after having had them for free for so many months, donated by local hiking clubs who loved the Appalachian Trail and its hikers.

If you chose not to pay ten dollars to sleep in a three-sided shack, then you could work for stay. I got to sift privy compost. I had hiked hard all day. I was pooped. I didn't want to filter decomposed human dooky. I wanted to sit in front of a sunset and breathe the crisp pine air. On days that I chose not to be a slave, I was forced to impact a pristine area, rather than sleep in an empty slot.

If you chose not to pay sixty bucks to have lasagna and bed sheets in the huts, then the AMC offered two work-for-stays. When we arrived at Mizpah Springs Hut, both openings were vacant, but there were three of us hoping for a night away from the bitter cold: Gizmo, Apple, and me. We begged for mercy to keep warm.

"We'll do extra chores. We'll sleep and not eat your food. We'll leave early."

The hut crew was merciless and demanded that one of us had to use the six dollar tent site. Eight scheduled guests had left over thirty empty bunks in the hut.

Apple braved arctic chills alone. His helping hands were not wanted. Gizmo gave him his bivy sack for extra warmth.

Work for stay? It wasn't a true work-for-stay. Gizmo and I were stuffed into the attic, where no guest ever stayed. There were four bunk beds available to choose from: one for Gizmo, one for me, and two... for nobody at all. Not for Apple. Not for anyone. We were asked to keep out of sight. No sleeping near the guests. No eating with the guests.

"Just stay upstairs or outside until they are done eating. Then you can come to the kitchen and help yourselves to the leftovers."

Were we loathsome hillbillies to whom no elitist would talk? We each had a story—a tale, which most people would have been delighted to hear—including anyone who could afford to pay full price at the dinner table. Certainly the guests had yarns to spin, too. We were treated like third-class citizens.

The AMC has nearly 100,000 members. Add to them paying non-members, and the number of thru-hikers is miniscule. But thru-hikers ranked high on the most-serious-hiker list. Nonetheless, thru-hikers either obeyed or were essentially told to "take a hike."

The White Mountains were spun with gossip and complaints regarding the AMC's treatment of thru-hikers. Not one thru-hiker I knew left AMC-Land without pins and needles about it. Superman summed it up well.

"The last welcome I received like that," he said, "was upon my return from 'Nam."

Trail Tidbit #64

Heavens to Betsy!

Ghosts? Who believed in ghosts? Between bites of cornbread, Gizmo told legends and scary stories. The Mizpah Spring Hut staff hung on his every word. I leaned against the kitchen stove and slurped my hot soup. Leftovers.

"Mizpah Hut has its own true ghost story," said the crew-guy. "The Legend of Betsy."

"Oh, yes! Tell them that one," said the crew-gal. She cranked two bulging eyes around to us. "This is freaky!"

"Back in the winter of 1971, some folks were hiking along the Dry River near here. A girl named Betsy fell through some ice and into the river—and drowned. A rescue team was called, and they recovered her body and put her in a body bag. Betsy was then stored in Mizpah Hut's basement, until they could get further help. When they came to pick Betsy up, the body bag's insides were shredded. Betsy had tried to get out!"

"She didn't actually die in the river!" said the crew-gal.

"That's right," said the crew-guy. "She had only swooned. They only thought she was dead. They thought wrong. She died in that body bag, consciously."

"And I'm convinced that this hut is haunted," said the crew-gal. Her eyes widened. "Down the hall, there's a picture on the wall of the 1971 Hut Crew, who helped get Betsy into the basement. That picture always hangs crooked. Whenever I walk by, I straighten it. One time I went into the room, next to where the picture hangs, to sweep the floor. When I came back into the hallway, the picture was crooked again."

"Spooky," I said.

Before bed I tipped the picture, so it hanged crooked on the wall again. The night was quiet: no ghostly footsteps, slamming doors, clinking chains, or whispering voices. Ghosts? Come on. Who believed in ghosts? Not me. There was a skeleton in my closet, however… Apple was probably shivering to the core outside, while I was snug inside. Selfishness haunted me until morning.

While the Hut's guests ate breakfast, Gizmo and I washed dishes in the kitchen. Suddenly, the crew-gal bolted in.

"The picture! It's crooked! The picture is tilted again!" she wheezed.

"Serious?" I asked.

"Yes! I swear!"

Ha ha ha. "Betsy!" I said.

We played along and followed her down the hallway.

"Wow! You're right," I said. "How freaky!"

The crew finished kitchen duties, while Gizmo and I swept the dining area, foyer, and hallway.

"Pst! Gizmo!" I whispered. "Look here!"

I opened my jacket. Tucked inside was the 1971 Crew picture. I put my finger to my lips and sneaked down to the basement, where the food storage was. I opened the refrigerator and set the picture on some cold meat. I wished I could have seen the crew's reaction when they found it, but we vanished after chores were done.

Ghosts? Who believed in ghosts? Not everyone. But some people could be *made* to believe in them. Betsy's ghost would surely live on. Now there was undeniable proof that she was real.

Rest in peace, Betsy. Let us do your dirty work. May your legend endure forever.

Above: I was on the Presidential Range in the White mountains, but who was I standing on this time?

Bottom Left: I watched from the attic in Mizpah Springs Hut, as paying vacation hikers ate a hot dish and talked about their day. I could smell the food and wished I could have joined them.

Bottom Right: Apple, Gizmo and I weren't staying at Lake of the Clouds Hut. Just taking a peek inside the AMC's highest hut. We hadn't seen Minstrel and Stormy for several days, but Apple just spotted their backpacks inside. Apparently, they and Tük, Sunny Campfire, Cannibal Pat and Pipline carried a girl with a torn ACL on a stretcher all the way up Mt. Washington. They were rewarded a free night stay at the hut. Nice, but they'll have to climb all the way back down to enjoy it.

Trail Tidbit #65
Cracked Cookie Case

"ey, Small World, did you get any cookies in your maildrop this time?"

"Yeah!" *Crunch, crunch, crunch.* "Peanut butter. Want one?"

Grandma's sneaky habit of sending cookies had become coveted common knowledge. I was the only hiker I knew of, whose grandmother sent fresh-baked goods. Each time she sent a batch, everyone including the postmaster got treats.

Maildrops were exciting. Remember the carrot? Maildrops gave me something to press towards, besides Katahdin. They gave me news from home, food, and surprises—like cards from friends or more of Grandma's cookies. They also were a great excuse to find a shower or ice-cream shop while in town. Pre-planned and well strategized, they could be a means to an End. Maildrops didn't, however, always come off as expected.

Jump back with me to Massachusetts. I was still with the Company. Apple and I had tuned our maildrops to the same towns.

"Guess what, guys?" I said to the gang. "I'm told there will be cookies waiting for us in South Egremont. It's a new recipe: gumdrop cookies with coconut."

"Rock on!" they cheered.

Apple and I pulled out our IDs at the post office and asked for our parcels.

One, two, three packages and an envelope came off the shelves. We stacked our treasure-boxes and brought them outside to shred open.

"Socks!" Apple shouted. "Two pairs! One for you, one for me!" It was a gift from his wife. Apple's brother, Bob, sent us each a supply of goodies in the second box: fruit bars, king-size Snickers, leftover Army MREs from the Y2K scare. The third box was mine. I ripped it open like a Christmas morning present.

"Uh, guys? No cookies," I mumbled.

"What?!"

"Sorry," I said, "I'll investigate."

I became the Gumdrop Gumshoe, determined to crack the missing cookie case. Beginning with the postmaster, I asked him to take another look around for me. Nothing. I needed more evidence. Tapping a line with my folks, I asked my mom if she had any clue of the cookies' whereabouts.

"Maybe Grandma sent them to your next drop in Cheshire," she said.

"According to her card, which I just opened, she sent the cookies here," I said. But I had a lead: Cheshire, Massachusetts.

Cheshire turned up two clues to the cookies' location. The first clue was that the cookies weren't *there*. Second, according to my sources, they were at Grandma's house again. How that happened, I could only hypothesize: they'd been shipped back.

Hm. At least they're safe. Now I have to figure out a way to return them to their rightful owners.

Another phone call later, I got a hint: "If you choose to accept, they'll be shipped in your next maildrop box."

Excellent.

We stole away for a while and landed in a village in Vermont called South Pomfret. The post office shared a building with the local grocery hub.

"Now, you're sure they're here?" Minstrel asked.

"Of course! I've got two packages," I said, weighing the evidence in my hands.

"Good. I'll buy milk."

I took the artifacts outside. Box number one was my regular maildrop. I knifed open box number two... cold weather gear, including my old backpack—the one I climbed Springer with. I bit my lip and looked up at everyone staring down at me.

"Uh, no cookies," I said.

"No cookies?!" Stormy squealed.

Minstrel glared at the milk carton in his hand.

Everyone sighed, as if to say, "Incompetent Inspector!" I assured them that I was the right sleuth for the job. We hashed out our next plan of action over a quart of milk.

I drew more data from my trusty source: Agent Mom. We were pointed northward, to North Woodstock, New Hampshire. Apple and I had to solve the dilemma alone, however. The Company would split within the following week. After several weeks together, Minstrel and Stormy were gone.

My data clarified that Apple and I would reach North Woodstock on Saturday night at the earliest. Sunday would close the post office. Monday would be Labor Day, when no one labored. We needed another plan.

As we neared NH 25, we met a southbounder named Ox. Apple reached him first and pumped him for clues before I showed up. I greeted them in my best British Sherlock accent.

"Small World, this is Ox," Apple said, "from England."

Wouldn't you know it? I felt like an idiot and immediately resumed an American Sherlock accent.

"Take a right on NH 25. Go down about a kilometer. Across from the post office, there's a home that boards hikers."

Perfect. We then had two alternatives. We could snag a twenty-dollar hitch from the homeowners into North Woodstock, or we could send a forward-mail request from the local post office to move our maildrops from North Woodstock to Gorham, New Hampshire. That was for free. We opted for the latter. That meant no cookies, again. I tipped Agent Mom not to send any more supplies to Gorham, since my North Woodstock maildrop should be forwarded there.

Now jump forward with me to Gorham, New Hampshire, past the Presidential Mountain Range in the Whites. We tracked down Gorham's postal building, as I examined the data:

> *Who: Cookies*
> *What: Missing*
> *When: Since August 10, 2000*
> *Where: To Hell and back!*
> *Why: United States Post Office Screw-ups and bad timing.*
> *How: Who knows, who cares? Just gimme my cookies, please!*

Apple and I flashed our IDs to the postal clerk. Private-eyeing my maildrop box, I slowly peeled back the packaging tape and peeked inside. Ramen Noodles. Powerbars. Dried veggies and fruit. Pop-Tarts. Oatmeal. Jerky. Vitamins. A cardboard carton.

"Apple, I think we've just cracked the cookie case."

"You got cookies?"
I tore open the carton.
"Got milk?" I said.
"Oh, hallelujah!" Apple howled.

Twenty-nine days and 357 miles after South Egremont, Massachusetts, we'd completed the impossible mission. It was cause for a celebration. We took a day off to celebrate our success at a small hiker motel with shots of milk and dozens of precious, satiating, and ever fresh-tasting homemade gumdrop coconut cookies.

Amazing pace,
My feet have found,
To savor crunchy tasties
Which once were lost,
Now safe and sound:
My grandma's long-lost pastries.

Trail Tidbit #66
Fortune Calls

Big Bald was so long ago. "What you see is what you get." The same fog greeted me at New Hampshire's Mt. Moosilauke. It had waited for me there. Moosilauke was the first mountain to rise above treeline, and I was eager to be there. What an upset it was! Then there was Franconia Notch. There was no place before Katahdin that I looked more forward to seeing than Franconia Notch.

The morning was blue and bright. I stood in the trees at the base of the mountain and wondered how long I would hike before reaching treeline. Several thousand steps later, the trees got scrawny and stunted. I could see the alpine ridge.

Yes. Yes! Look at that beauty! I was looking down on miles of yellowing trees and puffy clouds.

No. No! Wait! Stay away! A giant mass of clouds shoved its way over the ridge. It gulped me whole and spit my dreams out over a cliff.

I was livid. "What you see is what you get—my ass!" I couldn't *see* a thing! I felt like God was playing a joke on me. It wasn't funny. The fog hid the Trail, which was poorly marked to begin with. For miles I cursed and grumbled, until I got to a shelter.

"Ten dollars, please," said the AMC caretaker.

Ten bucks for a lousy shelter on a lousy trail? I thought. *No way!* Besides, I was low on cash with hundreds of miles to go. What made God's joke worse was that the skies had cleared by the time I stopped for the night. But I couldn't go and enjoy a vista. I had to sift privy compost to earn my sleep.

I think God felt bad. I didn't laugh at his joke, so he made up for it on Mount Washington. Two jet streams converge over Mount Washington, creating some of the world's worst weather. It is cloud covered 300 days of the year. Apple and I climbed it with 95-mile visibility. *Yes. Yes! Beautiful!* We would have clear skies until Maine. Thank heavens.

Five days on the Whites was exhausting, physically and emotionally. The Trail was rocky and hard to find, because white AT blazes or signposts were rare. Wind gusts were 40-50 mph. I clung to a cairn, as the wind blasted me like a bomb's aftershock. The descent into Pinkham Notch was death to the knees and seemed to last forever, even with our trail legs.

"I'm pooped," I said.

"That makes two of us," said Apple.

Gizmo added, "We have a choice to make. Either we can hitch from here into Gorham and take a zero day, or we can take the next access road—two days away."

Apple and I looked at each other.

"Grandma's cookies are there," I said.

"Gorham it is!" said Apple. Grandmotherly cookies were more enticing than the smothering mountain that followed. Plus I wanted to pick up my other backpack—the one I'd started with—for the rugged weather and terrain. Besides, I had it on Springer, I wanted it to go with me to Katahdin, too.

The Postmaster told Apple, "I have a note for you. A man called earlier, and he asked me to give you this message." He handed Apple a scribbled sheet of paper.

"It's my brother!" Apple exclaimed. "It says to call him before 5 p.m. *tonight*. He wants to drive up from Boston to see us."

We were flabbergasted. Grandma's cookies had saved the day. If it weren't for them, we wouldn't have come to Gorham until another two days and would have missed Apple's brother. We had finally learned to listen to our inner voices! Or was that our stomachs and aching feet we'd heard?

As soon as we found our room at the hiker hotel (Hiker's Paradise), Apple called his brother, and I opened my box of cookies. Grandma had wrapped each one in wax paper to keep them whole and fresh. Unfolding each one was like a hug. I whipped up some powdered milk to go with them.

Apple's brother arrived before ten o'clock.

"This is Randy," Apple (Roger) said.

I said, "Man, that makes what? Roger, Randy, Robert..."

"There's five of us," Apple admitted, "Ricky, Robert, Roger, Russ, and Randy!"

"Wow!" I said. "Your mom and dad took quite a bit of 'R-n-R', huh?"

"He was a farmer," Roger said. "He needed farmhands!"

That was what money was for on the Trail: a low-cost hotel with good friends, a Corona, chips, salsa, chitchat... and cookies.

Above: Wind speeds of 231mph have been recorded at the weather station atop Mt. Washington.

Bottom Left: I looked behind me, towards Georgia. I saw a thread draped across the ridge of the naked mountains—the Appalachian Trail. It looked so small. I am smaller yet, and my even-smaller feet crossed every stitch of that thread. I felt knitted into these hills.

Bottom Right: A cog train chugged up and down the mountain, carrying tourists and spewing thick black smoke into the what-would-be-pure mountain air. Tourists on board were known to spot strange sites in these mountains: such as hikers mooning them. It's practically a sport.

Wearing Fatigues

Webster's New World Dictionary says that a vacation is "a period of rest from work." Hiking the Trail was no vacation. The Trail was work. A week-long hiker once told me, "I'm just hiking on my vacation. I'm glad it's nearly over, so I can go back to work, where I can relax and take it easy!"

Dozens of people had asked, "How can you afford to take six months out of your life to do the Appalachian Trail?" The way I saw it, I was putting six months *into* my life, or at least putting *life* into six months of my life. How could I afford not to? It would be the hardest, yet greatest thing I'd ever done for myself.

In the beginning, my girth was without form and void of fitness. Fatigue bogged me down, begging for occasional zero-days to perk up again. But sometimes my spirits felt droopy coming out of town, even though my body was fresh again.

In the end-times, when trials and tribulations hit my body, I found a zero-day to be less healing—sometimes producing greater weariness. Getting back on the Trail was difficult not because we had no zeal to press on toward the goal, but because we were on the edge of total wipeout.

We were wearing thin. Blister Sister, whom I'd not seen for hundreds of miles said, "Small World! You get smaller every time I see you!" Apple was still following doctor's orders to fatten up his diet or face failure, but he was still losing weight.

After our zero-day in Gorham, New Hampshire, Apple and I felt like zombies under the spell of our backpacks. They were at their lightest weights yet, but felt heavier than ever. We dangled our thumbs in the air for a ride out of town.

"I'm really dreading Wildcat Mountain," I said. "My body is beaten, bruised and worn thin, like a boot in Pennsylvania."

"I remember Wildcat," said Gizmo. "What you've heard about it ain't rumors. It is steep."

"I'm just tired," Apple said.

"Why don't you guys share equipment and ship the rest home?" Gizmo said.

"It's Sunday," I said. "The post office is closed.

Gizmo had a solution for everything: "Ship it UPS from Rite-Aid Pharmacy."

So we did. Apple and I sorted our gear and decided to share a tent, stove, fuel, water filter, and boots (just kidding). We tossed everything but the bare essentials, splitting the weight between us. The difference in weight lifted our heels just enough to boost our attitudes. And rocky Wildcat Mountain went straight up.

"Wow!" I said, wiping my brow. "I feel good!"

"Me too," said Apple.

"I see a pattern here. The longer I'm out of town, the better I feel."

Apple replied, "It used to be, the longer we were out, the worse we'd feel!"

We stamped out a few more miles before nightfall. After dinner, I curled up in my sleeping bag inside Apple's tent, which I had carried. He kept the poles and rainfly in his pack. I began to play back memories from each State since March.

"Small World?" Apple whispered.

"Yeah?" I answered.

"Maine is right around the corner."

"I know..."

"Can you believe it?"

"Hm. I was just thinking about a man back home, who said I would never make it."

"We only have about 300 miles to go. That's gonna fly by. Then it's back to work—for a living, for money."

I lay there like a sack of wet rags, thinking about what Apple said. It made me feel tired and burdened. *Perhaps he was right. But why? Must it be so? Do I have to wear a blue or white collar again? I'd rather wear camouflage.*

"I feel so alive out here," I said. "Don't you? I mean, I feel as if I belong here. I wake up, do my routine, and go to sleep. Everyday. Out here, the routine is adventurous. I feel so at home now on the Trail. I don't want to leave. I am home."

"You need a woman," Apple said, laughing. "I've really begun to feel at home on the Trail, too, but I've got a new life to begin with my wife. I look forward to giving my marriage another shot."

"Don't get me wrong, Apple. I want to finish the Trail. I'm tired. But it's a different kind of exhaustion. I don't ever want to be as tired as I was before the Trail."

"Then take the Trail with you," Apple said.

My mind went numb. It was cold outside, and my eyes were feeling heavy. No more dreams of Maine. We'd *be* there tomorrow. I packed Apple's advice away, and went to sleep. I was tired.

Above: Bald Presidents stood tall and proud. **Bottom Left:** Finally, Grandma's cookies were in hand, in milk, in belly! I shared them with Apple, Gizmo, James and Veronica, whom I'd not seen since Virginia. I'd shaved off the rest of my scraggly facial hair to see if my double-chin was still there. Nope! **Bottom Right:** Near the last AMC hut, Carter Notch Hut, was a mesmerizing shallow lake, tinted red with its boulders. The hut hosted two "croo" members, their mothers, and two work-for-stay hikers. Despite bedspace, Apple, Gizmo and I were asked to bunk in the Great Cold Outdoors.

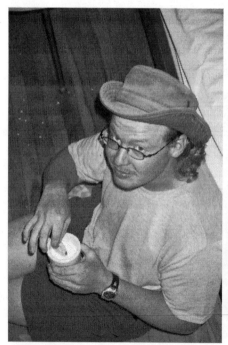

Trail Tidbit #68
Lost and Found

Crunch, crunch, crunch, crunch.

Both feet lost themselves in the autumn leaves.

My mind felt like a sieve.

"Tree, I'm at a loss for words—for thoughts."

Tree surrendered red, yellow, orange, and brown leaves to the nippy September air. But all words were held hostage.

"Tree?" I said.

A breeze whispered *Hush...*

"What? No more food for thought? No advice? No words of wisdom?"

Tree seemed to have gone mute. I decided to follow suit. No chatter. No hubbub. The metropolis between my ears had become a ghost town. *Ah*, it was nice.

After several hours, a feeling bubbled up in my chest. It wasn't heartburn. It erupted from my mouth. It wasn't gas. It was a burst of joy.

"I love this!" I exclaimed.

What?! howled Tree, laughing. I didn't know anyone had been listening. *What do you love?*

"Everything. The trees. The rocks. The loons. I love the Appalachian

Trail. I even love me!"

That was something I'd not heard myself say in a very long time. It was a feeling I'd not had in a long time. Love was like words on the tip of my tongue I'd longed to utter to a long lost loved one. It welled up within me—more than a sentence, it was an entire language. I yearned to share this feeling with someone else.

"If I had a woman, this language would well from my heart and pour from my lips onto her," I said. "Love, where have you been?"

Tree stood still. Not a word. Silence. But Tree didn't need to speak; silence spoke volumes. Love was the language. Love was loud. Love is a language louder than words. I knew this truth to be true. Truly true. I experienced it for myself. I was content, although I wondered what it would be like to share this love with another human being. A woman. Someday. I hoped. Someday. But for now, I was thankful for what I had. Beyond words.

Trail Tidbit #69
Moon No. 178

Journal Entry
9/21/00—From Cranberry Stream Campsite to West Carry Pond Lean-to
(20.7 miles)

I crossed the 2000-mile mark today, painted in yellow, right on a
country road we crossed.

The icy blue morning clouded over with rain while climbing Avery
Peak on the Bigelows. I started shivering and asked the skies to clear up, so
the sun could warm and dry me out. It did!

It's autumn, and the Trail is sprinkled with red leaves. From the
heights, I see a dazzling patchwork of trees: red, orange, yellow, brown,
green, burgundy, auburn, gold. While scaling an orange and red-covered
peak, I saw two southbound hikers ahead. It was B&B! When we saw each
other, Beth threw down her hiking sticks, and we squeezed each other.

B&B flip-flopped to Canada to do the International AT and are
hiking back to Harpers Ferry. Beth will be the first woman to do it, I
believe. She described how she and Bryant got to see whales cresting,
dolphins jumping, and many other spectacular sites along Canada's Trail.

They congratulated my success this far, and I wished them luck.

When I reached West Carry Pond shelter, it was full of hikers sitting in circle playing cards.

"Good evening!" I said, "Is there anyone I know here?"

"Hi, I'm Gigglebox."

"I'm Little Yellow Bird."

"Bullfrog."

"Wow!" I interrupted the roll call. "I've been following all your register entries for months! I can't believe I never ran into you until now."

"What's your name?" Gigglebox asked.

"I'm Small World."

"Small World!" exclaimed two other hikers whose backs had been to me, their turn to play their cards.

"Oh my go... Rising Moon! I don't believe it. It's been what, since Georgia?" I said.

"Yes, the night we each received our trailnames!"

I wonder what Rising Moon and his wife's (Yellow Jacket) story are. How many moons have risen since that night at Whitley Gap shelter in Georgia?

If all goes according to plan, only nine moons will rise before I reach Katahdin.

Trail Tidbit #70
Feature Creature

A ll animal aficionados along the AT anticipated an encounter with a mighty moose. The first sign of moose I saw was back in New Hampshire. It was located alongside US 3 in enormous yellow dots on a black background: WATCH FOR MOOSE!

I watched. I looked for morning moose, moose at lunch, and moose by moon. No moose.

"You'd think they'd be running rampant," I said to Apple. "With all these warning signs and all."

Yellow diamond-shaped signs with a silhouetted moose profile decorated every road crossing, warning drivers of ever-impending danger.

HUNDREDS OF COLLISIONS!

"Not something I'd brag about," I said. "It sounds like MacDonald's slogan: 'Billions and billions served!' Hey everyone—hundreds of collisions!"

"Perhaps that's where all the moose went," Apple said. "To the Golden Arches for lunch."

"Yeah, good point. Ten Billion *what* served?"

"Billions of moose served—to you—with fries on the side."

"Ew."

Moose signs of all sorts were scattered about: pellet piles, hoof-prints, heavy thrashing in the trees. But still no moose. Our first glimpse of a moose wasn't until Maine.

Five o'clock was our regular wakeup call, not only to make good use of narrowing daylight hours, but also to boost our chances of a moose sighting.

"Shh. Hike softly," Apple whispered.

I nodded.

The nippy morning mist around East Carry Pond hung like a still-life photograph. It was too cold for crickets or birds, so the world was mum. Finally, a marvelous, resonant tone rolled over the water. *Bwuuh!* I'd never heard a moose before, but I knew this was one. I could feel it. Halted in my tracks slack-jawed, I rapped on Apple's shoulder, shaking my head, as if to ask, "Did you hear that? Moose!"

We whipped out our cameras and tiptoed farther, until Miss Moosie Massive herself appeared. She was gorgeous. Another constipated *Bwuuh!* echoed off the water. Hiding behind the shore-side shrubs, we watched the cow graze the shallows just 50 yards away.

"Omigosh!" Apple whispered. "Look! To the left of her, camouflaged in the bushes. It's looking right at us."

My heart palpitated the Yen exchange rate, while every pore in my skin discharged currents of electric awe. We were being spied by a regal bull. The antlers crowned upon his head were his scepter and sword. His magnificence roared, "King of the North!" *Bwuuh-uh-uuh!*

Apple whistled an *Unbelievable!*

The King and Queen vanished into the trees. Their sheer size, capable of such graceful movement, was astounding.

Northern exposure was what these creatures were adapted to. In September, their furnaces were already lit to fend off temperatures that were potential death for Apple and me. Teenage temperatures sassed us every night and morning.

After breakfast in bed the next morning, we frantically stuffed our gear, as if we were going to miss a train. We were in a mad rush to keep warm. We were so fit, however, that we could be sweating within minutes.

Temperatures rose throughout the day. When we got too hot, we stopped to remove layers. Apple moved ahead, while I balanced my gear in my backpack. Then I propped my pack onto my back, buckled my waist belt. I could hear someone crunching in the leaves down the ridge-side to my right.

Hikers, I shrugged. *Probably coming back to the Trail after a pit-stop.*

I cinched down my shoulder straps and stepped forward.

Bwuuh! Bwuuh!

Moose! I thought. *Coming straight towards me. Oh, crud! Moose: fiercely territorial, sadly nearsighted.*

Neither did I yearn to be trampled to death, nor did I wish to be mistaken for gorgeous Miss Moosie Massive herself. I jumped behind the nearest tree and yanked out my camera. The zoom lens caught the bull's attention.

Uh-oh!

He focused on me, and I him.

He took several unnerving steps toward me.

Panic stepped onto the racing block, ready to sprint at the signal.

Oh, please no, no, no. I don't want to be minced meat. I don't want to be moose-raped. I don't want to be one of the hundreds of collisions.

The space between us tightened.

Nice moose, I thought as loud as I could. *Good moose. Friendly moose. Going-away-from-me moose. Not-attracted-to-me moose. Bored-with-me moose.*

Mr. Moose backed away and charged up the mountain. *Nice moose. Nice moose.*

I began breathing again. I was glad he didn't trample me. I was happy that he didn't find me sexy. I was thrilled that I was found to be a bore. No hurt egos. I'm a bore. Boring. Fine. As long as it kept Mr. Moose from playing with me. I galloped onward to find Apple. This was good news. I wanted to sing. Everyone should know my life was spared. Come, sing with me:

> *Go tell it on the mountain,*
> *over the hills and everywhere;*
> *Go tell it on the mountain,*
> *that moose was nice but bored!*

Top Left: We were glad to be out of AMC-Land and into the home of MATC (Maine AT Club). They built bog-walks, because the mud gets deep enough to disappear in, like quicksand. **Top Right:** I called for Apple to stop, so I could snap his picture. The sky was so clear, I said, "Boy, you look good in blue!" **Bottom Left:** Sherpa (whom I'd met as Scott in North Carolina) squeezes between a rock and a hard place in Mahoosuc Notch—known as the longest mile on the AT. **Bottom Right:** Maine's lakes and ponds were too cold for the skin, but soothing on the eyes.

Going Postal

A white AT blaze was painted on the floor of the canoe. We used the canoe to ferry across the Kennebec River.

"We need two days of food, Small World," Apple said, as he paddled. "That will get us to Monson, the last town before the 100-Mile Wilderness."

"The little town of Caratunk isn't far from here. We can get groceries there."

"Right. But how are we going to get our maildrops in Monson? It'll be Sunday when we get there. If we want to reach Katahdin by October 1, we can't wait a day more for the post office to open."

"We need all the time we can get. Let's ask the postal clerk in Caratunk if there is any way we can work it out."

The post lady in Caratunk called the Monson post office.

"...Yes, he's right here. Yes. Oh! How 'bout that? Sure. One moment, I'll ask," said the post lady. She put her hand over the receiver. "Mr. Welch, you weren't planning on staying at the 'Pie Lady's' house, were you?"

"I am," I answered.

"Well, she's at the Monson post office right now. Would you mind if she took your mail home to hold it for you?"

"That would be perfect!" I gawked at Apple.

"You gotta love small towns," Apple said, "where everyone knows everyone and cares."

The Pie Lady was expecting us (we had called her several days previous), so she agreed to take our boxes and envelopes home. She was an older single woman who invited hunters and hikers to meals and bargain lodging. And she made wonderful pies.

After a huge meal, we brought our mail to a small cabin in her back yard, where Apple and I watched the Olympics on a small TV and sorted through our maildrops. It was our last one. I was expecting a letter from my friend Ron, who planned on driving from Michigan to hike Katahdin with Apple and me. He was also my ride home. His letter would clarify his plans on where and when to meet us. But the letter wasn't with my stash. I telephoned him, but he had already left.

"He charted out all kinds of places to stop and enjoy the fall colors," his wife said. "You know him and his camera!"

There was nothing I could do but hope for the best.

During Sunday morning breakfast, someone knocked on the Pie Lady's door. It was a woman from the Monson post office.

"Good morning. Is Mr. Welch still here? I have some mail for him that came in after you left the post office yesterday."

It was Ron's letter.

Ah, small towns! They could be such sources of inspiration, like Olympic coaches goading their athletes toward the finish line. Monson was our last town on the Appalachian Trail, but they were first on the list of the most hiker-friendly. We left Monson feeling energized to tackle the 100-Mile Wilderness, and to watch for Ron.

No Rain, No Pain, No Maine

Journal Entry

9/25/00—From Monson, ME to Wilson Valley Lean-to (13.7 miles)

When I got to Monson, I was frustrated because of the rain. A thru-hiker named Wicked said that showers are expected for the next five days.

"It figures," I said. "Our last days on the Trail, through the 100-Mile Wilderness, will be rainy ones."

Wicked tried to heal our wounds. "Think of it this way," he said. "You'll probably get nice weather then for Katahdin." No doubt…

I called my family this morning, before we left Monson—the last time I'll be able to talk to them before Katahdin.

"Wouldn't you know it, Mom? It's supposed to rain all week," I said.

"Don't get dragged down by it," she replied. "These are your last days on the Trail. Go with a strong, cheerful spirit."

But how 'bout this—today was sunny! The Trail is rooty and rocky as usual in Maine, but at least the marshes are not overflowing, and the bog-walks are not all rotten (as they were in AMC-Land). I'm most happy for sunny skies, however. The night is in the 20s, and that doesn't mix well with wet clothes.

Fording Big Wilson Stream was the most painful experience on the AT yet. To lighten my pack, I'd sent my camp-sandals home from Monson. Wicked had told me that I wouldn't need them, anyhow. Wrong. I had to cross the stream barefoot. The creek-bed stones were round and slimy slick. I had to grip hard with my naked toes. Oh, it was cold! My feet kept jamming between the rocks, slipping while I tried to find footing. Each step was like balancing on a live electric wire. Pain jolted up through my legs, groin, and spine. Water crept up my legs and over my thighs, reaching "No-man's Land." I wobbled and nearly fell in. Finally, I reached the other shore.

I thought I had broken a toe. My shorts were soaked, and I started to shiver. I couldn't think—my feet and brain were numb. Apple rushed over to me and dried my legs off with his pack towel.

"You gotta change out of your shorts into dry clothes," he said. "Quickly."

We built a large fire at the shelter to warm up and dry out our clothes. Had I been hypothermic, Apple would have saved my life, acting the part of Brother's Keeper that I admired in him. I should thank my lucky stars. There are many of them out tonight. They're a part of my home on the Trail. Ceiling fixtures. Nightlights.

My home has become so comfortable. When I started building my home in Georgia, every task was a strain. I didn't have the skills. Now they're natural and familiar. I love my home. Apple is a good roommate. We share duties. No words are needed to throw camp together. The tent pops up and dinner is cooking within two minutes. It's so simple. Home sweet home.

Trail Tidbit #73
Informal Celebrities

Tree stared at me.

"One thing I'll never forget is how people affected my life on the Trail," I said.

Tree just stood there.

I continued, "I'll have to write a story about them and how they shared this chapter of my life."

Give me some examples, said Tree.

"In Cherokee, North Carolina, I stumbled upon a trinket and souvenir shop, which sold everything from toy tomahawks and arrow heads to authentic Cherokee relics. Roy, the storeowner, chewed my ear off for an hour, teaching me some Cherokee history. I studied his curled-up mustache, as a local walked in to buy cigarettes—a handsome Cherokee man with stereotypical Indian features and perfectly parted white hair. I stared at him as he lit up a cigarette and made small talk with my over-the-counter-teacher. After he left, Roy asked if I knew who he was. Of course, I didn't.

'That was Henry Lambert, the most photographed Indian alive,' he said. 'Even National Geographic has a story on him.' I was impressed.

I also got to meet Wingfoot."

I remember him, Tree said.

"I'm sure you do," I said. "He's hiked the Trail several times. Then there was Nimblewill Nomad. I met him first in Damascus and then again in Vermont. He's the first man to hike the entire Eastern Continental Divide. Someone told me that he had his toenails removed because of all the trouble they caused his walking."

Tree added, *Ah, yes. Nimblewill Nomad. Long gray hair. Thick bushy beard. Well-mannered, soft spoken.*

"Yes, that's him. Names and faces may fade, but I've met so many peo—"

"Hey, Small World!" Apple said, hiking up from behind. "Let's stop for water."

We sat at a spring together at the foot of East Chairback Mountain. Moments later, a southbound mother-daughter pair came to the spring with their rat dog Charlie.

"Hi, we're Charlie's Angels," the girl said. This was their first backpacking trip, and they were on their way to Georgia.

They're gettin' an awfully late start, I thought.

"We didn't know it would be this hard," the mother said.

"You ain't seen nothin' yet," Apple hooted, trying not to sound too discouraging.

The girl added, "And the 100-Mile Wilderness? There's no way to get food!"

"Not for a hundred miles," I said, not trying to sound sarcastic.

"Thank God for that man at Antlers Campsite. He's serving spaghetti and salad to hikers. Maybe you've heard of him. His name's Bill Irwin."

"Bill Irwin!" I blurted. "He was the blind man who thru-hiked with his dog, Orient, in 1990. He's a living legend. I can't wait to meet him."

"He's only going to be there for two more days," said the mother.

Apple and I crammed three days of miles into two, in order not to miss him. Upon arrival, his wife stood from underneath the canopy and greeted us, while Bill chewed the fat with a couple other hikers who were stuffing their faces.

"You guys want some hot spaghetti?"

Must I say it again? Does a hiker ever turn down foo— "Yes, please!"

Bill and Deborah had canoed over a lake with several days' worth of supplies: oranges, cookies, pink lemonade, salad, and spaghetti. Bill gave the blessing over the meal, and we ate several helpings. Bill regaled us with his Trail tales, settling all our question marks with—believe me—exclamation marks. It was an amazing nine months for him, all revealed in his book *Blind Courage*. Bill

Irwin was there to encourage, bless, motivate, feed, befriend, and congratulate hikers. That's what he did for me, anyway.

Hundreds of people's paths crossed on the Trail. It was the casual persons, living their lives on (or off) the Trail, which allowed me to be shaped by them, as well as the flowers, clouds, rivers, animals, rocks, and trees. My memory pulls up only a handful of flowers, and is rather foggy about the clouds. I can recall a Tree or two, but what I remember most about my journey, are the people I met—including myself.

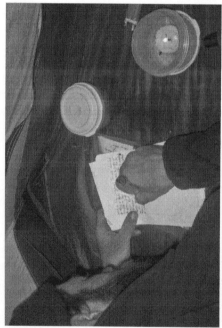

Top Left: Next to Sabbath Day Pond, Apple and I didn't use the shelter; it was warmer inside the tent together. While we journaled by candlelight, while loons sang on the pond.

Bottom Left: On Little Bigelow Mountain, I ran into B&B, whom I'd not seen since Virginia. Good friends, we threw our arms around each other.

Right: Fording rivers was easier with hiking poles, but painful nonetheless, as bare toes gripped the smooth rocks under the surface, and the near freezing water hugged our bodies with a death grip.

Trail Tidbit #74
Out of Sight, Out of Mind

Journal Entry
9/28/00—From East Branch Lean-to to Nahmakanta Stream Campsite (23.8 miles)

This morning was freezing. I threw my stuff together and got out of the tent as fast as I could. Apple gets around slower in the mornings, so I routinely pump out jumping-jacks to keep warm, until he's ready. I can't roll up my half of the tent until he's out of it.

Still no sign of Ron. He was going to leave a note for us at the Jo-Mary dirt road crossing, but we must have beaten him there. We left a note for him, instead.

Apple took the lead today. He's always been faster on ascents, and he scaled the mountain well ahead of me. When I reached the top, I saw a wooden sign with an arrow. "View" was all it read.

"Small World, com'ere!" Apple called. I followed the faint path until I saw him on a rock outcrop over a multicolored autumn view of Maine. I pulled out my camera to snap his picture. Apple turned around and looked at me. His eyes were lit up.

"What?" I said.

Apple reached up to pull the pine branch away, and he pointed his finger out over the vista.

"Look," he whispered.

I couldn't see what he was so wide-eyed about, so I walked closer. And I was stopped in my tracks. There she was! Big as ever, towering above every hill around her, tall and proud. Katahdin. The last big carrot dangling in front of us. It was an omnipresent fantasy for six months. Catching our first glimpse of "Special K" after 2,000 miles was like coming out of a coma. Katahdin means "greatest mountain." I witnessed her greatness. I choked up with tears. The realities of the Trail's end hit me hard.

Six months! How did I do it? There was a time when the thought of a thru-hike was simply bewildering. Daunting. Even more, now that I see what a thru-hiker goes through: all those miles, all the scenes, all the weather, all the pain and discomfort, all the joy and excitement, it boggles my mind. What kept me going?

I still remember Day One. It was the very day I had planned on from the beginning of my dream to hike the AT: March 28. Now it looks as if my chances are good to climb Katahdin on my birthday, October 1—just as dreamed. What a coincidence.

I'm ready.

How *did* I do it? I imagine that if I could see all the food I've ever eaten in my life, sitting in a pile before me, then I would ask the same question: "How did you do it? How in the world did you eat all that?!" That, I suppose, is the Trail: One bite—one step at a time.

Trail Tidbit #75
Endless Goal

Winter was coming. I shivered while Winter's chilling hands massaged my back and shoulders. Twenty-seven degrees. Must start hiking.

"Apple," I said, teeth clicking. "I have my half of the tent. I gotta go, I'm freezing."

"I'll catch up," Apple replied, stuffing his foot into an ice-coated boot.

Thirty minutes later, I wiped my brow with a bandana. It was good to be warm-blooded. My boots had thawed, and my legs and feet met the ground with intention to remain close friends. I had to make each step count—there weren't many left. A few thousand perhaps. Red leaves decorated the Trail and hung on pines like Christmas ornaments.

One snowflake. Two snowflakes. Three. I imagined what Maine would be like in the dead of winter. Millions of snowflakes for sure. Temperatures below zero. *Death*, I thought. Gazing around, I felt as if the land were preparing for a funeral.

Tree's voice sprang to life. *Some will die, but not all.*

"Thank goodness," I said.

Surely, death is not the End.

"What do you mean? I'm not so certain there's an afterlife, a Heaven," I said.

One thing we know for sure is that the Circle of Life does not only apply to plants and animals. Humans are not exempt. And if Heaven is real— if there is an afterlife—it wouldn't apply only to humans. What would the human spirit be without us trees?

"Spirit? Maybe there is no spirit. Maybe we're simply biomasses doing what biomasses do. I wish I knew. I want answers. Why is there nothing convincing? Why does faith seem unreasonable? I just want to know if there is a God or gods. I just want to know what happens in the End!" I said, grinding my hiking poles into the frozen turf.

There's one way to find out, said Tree.

I stopped in my tracks and looked at Tree sideways. "You mean to call it quits on life?"

What do you treasure more, Small World, answers or life? Tree asked.

I churned the dirt under my heel.

Tree continued, *Why haven't you quit the Trail yet, Small World? What brought you this far?*

"Insanity," I laughed. "Actually, I came to the Trail hoping to find answers."

So it was hope that kept you hiking. Hope for answers. Hope for understanding. Hope for new—

"Yes, although hope is a funny thing," I cut in.

"Funny" ha-ha? Or "funny" strange? Tree asked.

"Hope is insanity," I said. "Having hope is like playing the Lottery. Everyone hopes to win, but you're insane to keep trying, because your chances of losing are so high.

Yet if you don't play, you have no chance of winning. You kept hiking in hope for new life.

"Hm," I replied. "New life. That is something I have found. The past six months have been filled with it—dirty, raw, genuine life. It wasn't easy. Sometimes I was ready to be done. But I never could have quit. I loved new life too much."

The goal of the Appalachian Trail is not Maine, Small World. The goal is the journey. All six months of it. The End is not the point of the Trail. The pilgrimage is.

"The End is near, Tree," I said.

But life goes on, Tree said, *trust me. You will take the Trail with you: the things you accomplished, the things you felt, the things you learned.*

"I learned a lot, but I thought I would finish the Trail with greater faith," I said. "I never thought I'd leave agnostic. Even what you tried to teach me sits in a puddle of question marks."

What I taught you were not necessarily truths *to be believed, but rather* ideas *to help you climb outside the box that was given to you to thrive in. One lesson I did intend for you to believe: the sacredness of all things: rain, mountains, valleys, open fields, forests, rocks, ponds, the community of life—*

"That lesson I believe now, because I've experienced it. I've tasted it myself."

Take it with you. Life—it's what will save your life. Life begets life. Being agnostic with life and joy in your heart is better than being bitter and frustrated with all the answers. Besides, with a healthy heart you can continue to spend your lifetime looking for answers.

"Tree," I said. "If the mystery of the universe were solved, what would be left to live for?"

I dare say that if these questions are answered, there will be ever more questions to ask. If not, however, I should imagine that the only thing left to live for is life itself. To see where it takes us. To hope. To evolve and grow and change is what life is about. Life isn't about the End. It's about the journey.

"Yes, of that I'm convinced," I said. "I may be insane, but I'm convinced."

Above: In the heart of Maine, it pumped its blood into my veins, filling me with enchantment.

Bottom Left: The glassy river reflected the mood of the forest. They can be deceptive, too, when fording. Their rocks can wobble when hopping across, and their depths are often deeper than I expected. My hiking poles were useful for measuring depths, as well as for balance.

Bottom Right: Bill and Deborah Irwin at Antlers Campsite.

Trail Tidbit #76
The Final Countdown

Journal Entry
9/30/00—From Rainbow Lake to Daicey Pond Campground (15.3 miles)

While we fell asleep last night, loon calls filled the sky around Rainbow Lake. I think they were bidding farewell.

Apple and I cleared the 100-Mile Wilderness today. Mileage that took us two weeks to hike in the beginning, we did in five days. We've had blue skies since Monson. The Daicey Pond Campground Rangers say the conditions to climb Katahdin should be just as lovely as today's weather. I'm so thankful. I don't think we would have made it here by now, if it weren't for the fantastic weather.

Still no word from Ron. I must find him. It's his dream to climb Katahdin, too. And he wants to take pictures of my last steps to the sign on Katahdin's peak.

At Abol Bridge Campground's store, Apple and I bought a couple bottles of suds (Katahdin Beer) and toasted our success on a boulder on a nearby river under the warm sun.

I can hardly believe tomorrow is it—the final summit! My

enthusiasm is stuck to the bottom of my boots, and I can't get it off. I suppose I don't want this to end. This is my home. This is my life. The Trail has become my castle of refuge and strength, welcoming friends, providing peace. I traveled a great distance to find my home—on the Trail and within myself.

Perhaps I'm tired. I must rest, so that I have the energy to climb with full joy tomorrow. I'm a bit nervous about it. Anxious, yet eager. I know that I will soar with enthusiasm when I wake up in the morning. Then again, will my thoughts be on the fact that I have to return to the Real World? No, wait. This *is* the Real World. It's no less real than Man-land. If anything, it's more real. It's just modest and speaks softly.

Katahdin. I heard it whispering all day—all week—beckoning me. Now I whisper back, "Here I am!"

Above: The day before our final summit, Apple and I sat pensively at Daicy Pond to reflect.
Bottom Left: Katahdin Stream Falls—I wondered where it came from and where it was going.
Bottom Right: The next five miles to the top would be our last, but we smiled nonetheless.

Above: Mt. Katahdin.

Bottom Left: Apple, as usual, always looked up.

Bottom Right: I felt hard as stone physically and mentally. But emotionally, I was soft and subtle that last day. Above treeline, I soared, yet was humbled to think of the terrain of my life the past six months.

Far From Home

Beep-beep. *Beep-beep. Beep-beep.* I pushed the button on my wristwatch to turn off the alarm. It was 5:00 a.m. and still dark. I'd been awake for a while now. Apple was still sleeping, but the forest was waking up.

Good morning, whispered Tree.

"Good morning. My last morning. It's so quiet," I said, not loud enough for Apple to hear.

There were no birds, no buzzing flies, no breezes. Tree stood still.

"This is it," I said with a sigh. I bit my bottom lip.

You'll do well, said Tree.

I tapped Apple on the shoulder to wake him. He looked up at me without a word. The look in his eyes said it, too: "This is it." We packed camp in silence.

I was first to break the icy morning: "Apple. I've got to leave. Maybe I can find Ron at the foot of Katahdin in Baxter State Park. He could be at the campground there."

"Go," Apple said. "It's just over two miles. We've got time."

"I'll meet you there, buddy."

I followed the white blazes around misty ponds and red maples. My mind suffered under the weight of the hundreds of carrots I'd collected over the past six

Above: My friend, Ron, had waited many years to have the chance to climb Katahdin.

Bottom Left: Katahdin was more technical than we'd expected; hand-over-hand climbing was made easier with steel rods bolted into some boulders to hold onto.

Bottom Right: Apple and I ate a snack at the bottom of the last section before the plateau and peak, while we waited for Ron to catch up.

months—so many Trail memories. Those two miles were like a long goodbye.

Will I ever return home? I thought.

The Trail emptied out onto a lost dirt road. The white blazes followed it to the Katahdin Stream Falls campground. It was barely daybreak, but I could see a few people rummaging around their campsites, preparing for the day's hike. I stepped aside to let a mini-van pass. The van stopped and the driver-side window hummed open.

"It's a small world, after all," said the driver.

"Ron!" I yelled.

"Need a ride?" he asked. Ron was just leaving to look for me.

I stretched through the window and hugged him.

Apple arrived twenty minutes later.

"You guys taking your backpacks with you to the top?" asked Ron.

"Wouldn't leave home without it," I said.

My Lowe Alpine backpack was a good friend, and it deserved to see the summit with me. Nevertheless, Apple and I dumped most of our gear into the van to make our packs lighter. We tightened our straps and laces and posed for pictures with Mt. Katahdin shining in the morning light behind us.

"You guys do your thing," Ron said. "I'll never be able to keep up. Don't let me slow you down."

"There's no hurry," Apple said.

"Right. We'll make it last," I said. It was as if Ron was a guest in my home. I felt as if it would be polite to hike at his pace. Besides, I wasn't looking forward to sitting in a car for hours on end anytime soon.

Apple and I entered the trees together. Ron clicked photos behind. The higher the Trail went, the rockier and more rugged it became. When Apple and I had marched too far ahead of Ron, we waited.

"I can't imagine how this must feel to Ron. I couldn't have done this six months ago!" I said.

"There he is," Apple pointed.

"How ya feeling, Ron?" I called.

"Like I'm going to puke," he answered.

"Take a break," said Apple. "We'll wait here with you. Take your time."

After a few swigs of water, Ron was ready to go. The trees thinned and became scraggly. We were nearing treeline. I loved trees. I had learned so much from them. I recalled that pine tree in Massachusetts and the other one in Virginia, whom I'd talked with. They were still there, surely. Happy. Did anyone else know that? Would anyone *ever* care?

"Good old Tree," I whispered.

This is it. It was the voice of Tree. *One last carrot in this carrot patch.*

"Goodbye, Tree," I whispered, "and thank you. You've all been good friends." I pressed my lips together to hold back tears.

Small World, Tree said. I turned toward that last tree in the rocks. *Happy birthday.*

A tightlipped smile creased my face, and my brow furrowed. My feet returned to their rhythm. White blazes were painted on boulders, down low and up high. I gripped the boulder above me and heaved myself up. Left, right, left, right. Muscles rippling. Boots crunching. Mind freeing. Spirit soaring! I was on top of the world—the carrot top!

Right, left, right, left... Apple and I marched side-by-side a mile high, leaving in our trails the only offering we had to give to Katahdin: reminiscence. Trail stories. Memories. Laughter. Pain. Friendships. Lost friends. Questions. Answers. Hopes. Dreams. And more laughter.

Katahdin was such a dreamy word for months. Now was it possible that I'd come this far? These legs? These feet? They say it takes about five million steps to complete a thru-hike. I still recall the last five steps.

Two steps to go. One step to go. The last white blaze. The sign at the fingertips. I held the sign. Time stood still. It ended much like it began. Quiet. Pensive. There was no applause, no trumpets—just the gentle voice across the wind, *You did it.*

Then our shouts of joy and accomplishment echoed through those mountains. Ron snapped our photos at the sign. Apple and I took time alone to sit at the peak to gaze and think. I looked southward. I was sure Georgia was still there, over 2,167 miles away. I took a deep breath. *What a birthday present,* I thought. I felt born again.

It was October 1, 2000—my birthday. I did it.

*If one advances confidently
in the direction of his dreams
and endeavors to live his life
which he has imagined,
he will meet with a success
unexpected in common hours.*

HENRY DAVID THOREAU

Post Trail Tidbit
Ever After

My travels brought me to my home away from home. It took time to adjust to the cars, lights, concrete, and noise of civilization. Sensory overload. Civilization is a wonder in itself, though. What an invention! Who thought of it? How did we make it? One step at I time, I suppose—like the Trail.

I miss the Trail. I miss my home there. I miss waking up to new scenes and sounds every day. I miss job hiking and making camp. I miss my friends.

Back in Duncannon, Pennsylvania, I had taken a room at a truck stop, where I'd found a leftover fortune cookie from the previous tenants. The fortune had foretold that I would soon be in a new home.

"How ironic," I'd laughed. "I'm in a new home every night!" Little did I know that I would type the first draft of this book under the roof of a gorgeous home ten minutes away from a Florida ocean. It wouldn't be my home, however. I would be house-sitting for Lady Kat, with whom I had climbed Springer Mountain.

Apple and I keep in touch over the phone. He is happy with his wife in their new home.

Ring. Ring.

"Hello?" I said.

"It's a boy!"

"Apple! Congratulations!" I screamed. "What's his name?"

"Zachary."

Apple and I keep each other posted on news about people we knew on the Trail.

"Did you hear that Beth, from B&B, finished the Eastern Continental Divide Trail?"

"Did you hear that Cool Hand Luke and Fennel are getting married?"

"How about Fenway and Nails? They're getting married, too."

"Superman's mother-in-law died."

"Gizmo is the caretaker on Springer Mountain now."

"Minstrel went to California to pursue a music career."

"What about you, Small World?" asked Apple. "Are you still thinking about hiking across America?"

"No," I answered. "I met a girl here in Florida, while house-sitting for Lady Kat. I decided to stay."

"What's her name?" Apple asked.

"Debra."

Home is where the heart is. My heart is with Debra. After two thousand miles, my journey continues with her. Now she is my mountaintop vista. She is my breath of fresh air. Debra's brown eyes reflect my true self, making me a better man. Debra is living water when I thirst for love and peace. She has the heart of a mountain and the voice of a Tree.

I write this book for her, because the Appalachian Trail led me to her. The journey endures through her. Debbie, you are my Springer and my Katahdin. You are my dream and my hope. We have proved our love for each other through valleys and over peaks. We have seen each other under sunny skies, as well as under cloudy, rainy ones. But there is no *bad* weather.

Right now we're sitting on the beach under the stars. I have shared this book with you over the past several days. You've read to me. I've read to you. Now I'm burying my toes in the sand while you read these last words. This is it. There is no applause, no trumpets. Just you and me. The Trail is behind me. You sit before me. Look at me, my love. I have a ring in my hand. Will you marry me?

We were long-distance friends.

People to Thank
Acknowledgements

Trail magic is everlasting. Eight years after my Appalachian Trail, not one day has sneaked by without remembering it. I am thankful for all it means to me, but one thing I learned upon writing this book is that the Trail was about people, including yours truly. Not only could my journey not have been accomplished without *me*, but also it would not have been as successful without the fabulous persons along the way. Although I cannot mention all of them, may this book honor their inclusion in my journey from Georgia to Maine.

My journey was what it was, partly because of my friends and family who sent me letters, cards and care-packages: my sisters, Melanie and Mandy, Grandma; my friends Wolfgang and Terri (who set my feet at the beginning with a Greyhound ticket to Georgia), Matthew, Nathan, Clay, Val, Cherie, Karen and Pinny, Barbara, Gayle, John, Steve, Esther, Rich, Marci (who gave new eyes, when I'd lost my glasses), Tony, Jeff and Kathy, Karin and Norbert, Christoph, Virginia (who taught me to love trees), Ron and, of course, everyone on the Appalachian Trail—the AT Class of 2000.

I'm thankful to Dan "Wingfoot" Bruce's online Trailplace (www.trailplace.com) for the instruction and preparation. Thanks to Laurie Potteiger at the ATC for her work and hospitality. And thanks to Kathleen (Lady Kat) for her home, where I found rest and recovery, and to my best man, Roger (Apple) and Jennifer his wife, for being there along my way.

I'm most thankful to my parents, who cheered for me each step of the way, through every up and down. They perfectly organized my maildrops, sneaking in notes and goodies. My mom, especially. She was my cheerleader. She was the angel who watched over me the whole way, counting my steps. She was the first person I hugged when I got home.

Finally, I thank The Rockford Squire newspaper for allowing me to share my journey with the town I grew up in. Thanks to the Squire and all its readers, especially Lynn Macintosh, Aunt Holly and Liz Kells, who helped me to believe not only that I had a story to share, but also the ability to write it.